MARION FREYER WOLFF

D0711555

THE SHRINKING CIRCLE

Memories of Nazi Berlin

1933-1939

UAHC PRESS · NEW YORK, NEW YORK

Front Cover: Marion Freyer in first grade, Berlin, April 1932.
Historical photos, courtesy of the Leo Baeck Institute, New York, photos by Jim Strong.
Personal family photos of Eva Lichtenstein Freyer and Leo Freyer, the author's parents,
   by Z. Mandelstam.
Copies of original personal photos and documents by Jason Zuckerman.

Library of Congress Cataloging-in-Publication Data
Wolff, Marion Freyer.
   The shrinking circle : memories of Nazi Berlin, 1933–1939 / by
Marion Freyer Wolff.
      p.   cm.
   Bibliography: p.
   Includes index.
   Summary: A memoir of the author's girlhood in Nazi Berlin during
Hitler's rise to power.
   ISBN 0–8074–0419–5
   1. Wolff, Marion Freyer—Childhood and youth—Juvenile literature.
   2. Jewish children—Berlin (Germany)—Biography—Juvenile
literature.   3. Jews—Berlin (Germany)—Persecutions—Juvenile
literature.   4. Berlin (Germany)—Biography—Juvenile literature.
[1. Wolff, Marion Freyer—Childhood and youth.   2. Jews—Germany—
Biography.   3. Holocaust, Jewish (1939–1945)]   I. Title.
DS135.G5W63   1989
940.53'18'092—dc20
[B]
[92]   89–5140
                                                              CIP
                                                              AC

To the loving memory of

Leo Freyer (1893–1987)
Eva Lichtenstein Freyer (1895–1987)
Ursula Freyer Mandelstam (1921–1975)

my parents and sister who were able to come to America
and die in freedom

and

to the relatives and friends we had to leave behind.
They and the vibrant Jewish Community of Berlin
of my youth will forever live within me.

Acknowledgments

In writing this book, I relied to a large extent on my memory. The events that left their mark on my childhood and subsequent development are deeply engraved on my mind. In 1934 I had begun keeping a notebook, and I occasionally referred to its entries. My husband, John, who had been a fellow student at the Zickel School, helped me recall some of the events of the years 1936–1939. My father provided important information concerning our emigration. Correspondence with former teachers, classmates, and childhood friends helped fill the gaps in my memory. In order to verify facts and dates, I consulted many books, especially the Yearbooks of the Leo Baeck Institute.

Special thanks go to Rena Cohen Kelly, who critiqued the original draft of the manuscript, and to the groups of students and adults who invited me to discuss my experiences with them. A vast amount has been written on the period that I describe; yet, each individual was affected in a unique way. I decided to record my story for my daughter, Rebecca, and other young people in the hope that it will answer some of their questions and add to their understanding of our past.

I am grateful to the Union of American Hebrew Congregations for publishing my story and to Aron Hirt-Manheimer, my patient and supportive editor, for his guidance and encouragement.

Bethesda, Maryland   *Marion Freyer Wolff*
June 1988

Contents

Preface   vii

   I · 1933   1

  II · SCHOOL DAYS   4

 III · LEHNITZ   8

 IV · YELLOW BENCHES   12

  V · 1936: A JEWISH SECONDARY SCHOOL
FOR BOYS AND GIRLS   15

 VI · SPORTS   19

VII · THE SYNAGOGUE   26

VIII · 1937   30

 IX · CULTURE   35

  X · CHANGES   40

 XI · EMIGRATION   44

 XII · THE NUMBERS GAME   50

XIII · LIFE GOES ON   57

XIV · KRISTALLNACHT: THE NIGHT OF THE BROKEN
GLASS   62

 XV · FAREWELLS   68

XVI · FATE   72

XVII · DISSOLUTION   75

XVIII · KNAPSACKS   81

XIX · MOMENTUM   87

XX · WAR   94

XXI · THE LONGEST DAY OF MY LIFE   100

XXII · HOW DO YOU LIKE AMERICA?   106

Epilogue   112

Important Dates   117

Bibliography   121

Poem Recited by Ulla
at Her Confirmation, May 1937   124

Glossary/Index   127

Preface

Rebecca used to say to me, "Mom, you are so strange. Sometimes you make a big fuss about little things, but, when it comes to the big things, like real crises, you are so strong. I can't figure you out!"

Rebecca hasn't said that to me lately. She says she can understand me better since she's listened to the tapes. You see, about two years ago, a lady came to my house to tape my memoirs for the Oral History Project, undertaken by the Jewish Community Council of Greater Washington to record the experiences of Holocaust survivors and liberators.

I had prepared myself for this interview. My old identity card (No. 01.494997), the one with the fingerprints and the photo with the left ear exposed, was on the table. There was also a letter from a non-Jewish friend, written after the war, describing in detail the deportation of my aunt and my grandmother from Berlin. The friend had helped my grandmother pack her little suitcase. It was my grandmother's seventy-ninth birthday (October 15, 1942), and the next day she was pushed into a truck and never heard from again. Four months later my aunt was seized where she worked as a slave laborer, making iron chains, and deported to Auschwitz.

But my mind wandered as I recalled my lost relatives. The lady with the tape recorder asked me all kinds of questions, and I answered them in great detail. When she left, after more than two hours, I felt shaky and exhausted. After more than forty-five years in America, I still cry when I think about the Holocaust.

As I get older and realize the enormity of the destruction, the sense of loss becomes greater. When I was younger, I was too busy "getting on with my own life" and raising a family. Now I can take the time to review history and try "to come to terms" with it.

Rebecca, I will never be able to come to terms with it. When you were little and got into mischief, wise friends would say, "She only wants to attract attention." Rebecca, can you imagine a little girl whose greatest desire was *not* to call attention to herself? When the storm troopers marched down the streets of Berlin, one was supposed to stop and raise one's right arm in the Hitler salute. Often, on the way home from school, I would encounter these parades. It would have been so easy for me to stop and raise my arm when the flags went by. But I just couldn't do that. I would dodge into a store or the lobby of an apartment building, sometimes a stairwell or a small backyard, hoping that the drummers and marchers would pass so I could emerge from my hiding place before someone detected me. If only I could have gotten hold of a *tarnkappe,* "an imaginary hat that makes its wearer invisible"!

My father often had reminded me that it was important not to appear different in any way. "Never call attention to yourself," he would say. And so, when I had to report to the police to be fingerprinted for the ID card (March 20, 1939), he reminded me to hide the large scar on the left side of my neck. "When the officer asks you if you have any distinguishing marks, you must say no," he advised me. I pulled the turtleneck as high as I could and said no when the question was asked. I feared that the man would notice the scar, and I felt guilty at having lied.

Only Jews were issued these identity cards, which were printed on heavy oilcloth and had a large *J* on the front. The law required that I carry the *Kennkarte* at all times, ready to present it to a policeman or a Gestapo agent upon request. If you did not have the card, you were breaking the law and subject to arrest. On the other hand, if you did show the card, you revealed that you were a Jew, and there was no telling what harm might be inflicted on you or your family. So there I was, only thirteen, in a dilemma, which had no logical solution.

The lady with the tape recorder had prepared a list of questions to ask me. "Let's start at the beginning," she said. I put the identity card and the letter aside and began to tell her the story of my childhood in Berlin.

I

1933

Adolf Hitler came to power on January 30, 1933. I remember it all so well: We were sitting around the little wooden radio, listening to the *Fuehrer* speak. I put my hands over my ears in fear. His was not a human voice; it sounded like the shrieking of a mad animal. I couldn't understand what he was saying, but, from the threatening tone, I guessed it couldn't be anything good. My parents tried to calm me. "Don't worry," they said. "This will pass. We've been through hard times before." I wanted so much to believe that they were right, but, as the days passed, I realized that my fears were justified.

My family lived in Friedenau ("meadow of peace"), a working-class suburb of Berlin. Small shops lined its main street. After school, my mother would take me along to the dairy store, the bakery, the greengrocery, or to other shops in the business district. My favorite was Mr. Brie's sewing and knitting store, located in a corner building. Often, Mr. Brie, who was Jewish, stood at the door to welcome customers. He called me by my name and always had a pleasant comment. As he chatted with my mother, I would survey his collection of ribbons and laces and stacked bolts of cotton material. I was always drawn to the display of colorful buttons for I knew from where they had come. My father owned a small factory near the center of Berlin where he manufactured buttons and buckles. When Mr. Brie needed to stock his shelves, he would order the merchandise from my father. Business was good. Most of the neighborhood women did their own sewing, and the schoolgirls depended on Mr. Brie for their needlework supplies. In the afternoon the aisles of the store were crowded with mothers and children.

One afternoon (April 1, 1933), my mother and I set out to shop. As we turned onto Main Street, we became aware of a commotion. Dozens of uniformed Nazi soldiers were parading back and forth in front of the Jewish stores, carrying large posters proclaiming: Germans! Strike Back! Do Not Buy from Jews! Huge Jewish stars had been smeared in yellow paint on the store fronts, together with obscenities such as Jewish Pig and Filthy Jew.

I drew closer to my mother. I wanted so much to enter Mr. Brie's store, to show him that such scare tactics would not work. My mother must have read my thoughts. Slowly she pointed to a large sign above the entrance. It read Jewish Business! Whoever Buys Here Will Be Photographed. I noticed a uniformed man with a camera. Nobody stopped or made any attempt to cross the picket lines.

We turned into a side street. "Let's go home," my mother said. "All the stores are closed today. Soon the Nazis will go away, and then the shops can reopen. In a couple of days, we'll do our shopping at Mr. Brie's store."

The next week, the doors of my favorite store were open again, but Mr. Brie was not standing near the steps to welcome us. We found him in his back office. He looked sad and spoke in a low voice. Within one year he was forced out of business, and my father had lost one of his best customers.

The Boycott of 1933 marked the beginning of the systematic choking of Jewish businesses in Germany. The garment trade, which was predominantly Jewish, was especially affected. My father had worked hard to build up a button manufacturing business during the financial upheavals of the 1920s and 1930s—runaway inflation followed by worldwide depression. He was just beginning to experience some success when the Nazi Boycott of 1933 and other restrictive economic measures gradually deprived him of his livelihood. By 1937, his non-Jewish customers were no longer allowed to buy from him, and most of his Jewish clients had lost their businesses. When the Nazis seized the factory in 1937, our family slid from a middle-class existence into poverty. My parents rarely discussed their worries with my older sister, Ulla, and me. We felt sheltered and surrounded by their love. We lacked material comforts but enjoyed games, hikes, and music. Within our family, as Jews among Jews, the children did not feel deprived. And that security enabled us to face the outside world, the life of Jews among Nazis.

II

SCHOOL DAYS

In April 1933, I entered second grade at the local public school. Of the forty-five girls in my class, only two were Jewish—Ursel, who was younger than I, and I. Ursel's mother was a Hebrew teacher who taught me the Hebrew alphabet and the Ten Commandments. For many years Ursel and I were "best friends," not only because we liked each other, but because, with few exceptions, the other children in the class participated enthusiastically in the Hitler Youth movement and were taught to shun us. Ursel and I were outcasts, but we had each other, our secrets, and our private holidays.

At the beginning of the school year, each student had to stand up and answer a set of questions. The answers were noted in the class register, a large book on the teacher's desk. My father had prepared me to answer the questions so as not to call attention to myself. Miss Pfefferkorn asked each student about her date of birth, her address, her father's name, his occupation, and the family's religion. Most of the children answered, "Evangelical" (Lutheran); some answered, "Catholic"; and, when my turn came, I said, "Mosaic." Ursel listened carefully, and, when her turn came, she whispered, "Mosaic." "Speak up!" called the teacher. Ursel repeated, "Mosaic." I glanced at my classmates. Most looked bored. I prayed that they hadn't heard our replies or were unaware that Mosaic meant Jewish. After these introductions, we were issued our textbooks, and the lesson began.

Hitler did not lose any time in indoctrinating the young. The Burning of the Books (May 10, 1933) sent a clear message to all that any criticism of the Nazi world view would not be tolerated. All textbooks were censored or rewritten.

One day the teacher asked us to place our books on our desks. She then wrote a list of numbers on the board. These were the numbers of the pages that we were to tear out. She did not tell us why we were mutilating our textbooks, and nobody asked. She collected the loose pages and counted each sheet to make sure the forbidden words had been removed.

I had been taught to respect books. My grandmother had told me that a dropped prayer book had to be picked up and kissed. I had seen her do it in the synagogue. We were never permitted to mark a page or turn dog-ears in any book. Tearing out whole pages seemed so sinful.

Upset and confused by the teacher's demand, I showed the injured books to my parents. My father explained that we had many books at home that would never be hurt. But, in school, there were different rules, and they had to be followed. "You must not believe everything they tell you in school," he said. "At home we will tell you the truth, but in school you will be taught many lies. Do not call attention to yourself by questioning anything." He then turned to my mother and said quietly, "Marion is such a serious and sensitive child. She will have a very hard life."

I realized then that, in order to survive in the public school, I would have to lead a double life with two conflicting standards of behavior—at school as a Jew among Nazis, at home as a Jew among Jews.

This dual existence required ingenuity and self-control. Outwardly, I had to conform to the rules while inwardly trying to maintain my ethical standards. I soon learned that open defiance would backfire and that other ways had to be found to resolve the conflicts that would arise.

I cannot say with certainty that Miss Pfefferkorn was a true believer of the Nazi doctrine. As a state employee, however, she was obligated to follow the party line. And so the traditional greeting of "Good morning, Miss Pfefferkorn!" "Good morning, girls. You may be seated," was replaced with the Hitler salute. When the teacher entered the room, the students stood up, raised their right arms, and, in military fashion, called out "Heil Hitler." I kept my arm down and remained silent; Ursel saluted Hitler along with the rest of the class. Miss Pfefferkorn noted my disobedience but said nothing. At the end of the week, I was summoned before the school principal, who warned me that it would be in my best interest, and in the interest of my parents, if I would cooperate from now on. I remembered my father's admonition ("Never call attention to yourself") and nodded my head. I was allowed to return to the classroom.

The next day, I stretched out my arm with the rest of the class. But, when I said "Heil Hitler," it was not to honor the dictator. In German, the word *Heil* can mean "Hail to" or "May you heal." By endowing the salute with the second meaning, I could pray every morning that God should heal Hitler of his madness. This was my way of solving the conflict of my dual existence, enabling me to keep my self-respect.

There were some rare occasions when I actually managed to triumph over my environment. I remember one instance in particular in the fourth grade. Miss Pfefferkorn, who had remained our homeroom teacher throughout the four years of *Grundschule* ("elementary school"), had asked each student to learn a patriotic poem by heart. I decided to memorize Friedrich von Schiller's inspiring words from *William Tell* in which the priest calls on the people to take a sacred oath to unite, renounce tyranny, and choose death over servitude. I had rehearsed the words carefully, emphasizing those that were particularly dear to me.

When the day came, one girl after another recited verses extolling the virtues of blind obedience to the fatherland. At last, my turn came. I rose to my feet, my heart pounding loudly, and declaimed with fervor:

Wir wollen sein ein einzig Volk von Bruedern,	We want to be a united nation of brothers,

In keiner Not uns trennen	Never to separate in distress
und Gefahr.	or danger.
Wir wollen frei sein,	We want to be free,
wie die Vaeter waren,	as our fathers were,
Eher den Tod! als in der	We would rather choose death
Knechtschaft leben.	than live in slavery.
Wir wollen trauen auf	We want to put our trust
den hoechsten Gott	in the highest God
Und uns nicht fuerchten	And not be fearful
vor der Macht der Menschen.	of the might of men.

The class listened in awe as I concluded my presentation by saying, "These words were written by Friedrich von Schiller, one of the greatest German poets." The teacher seemed impressed. She nodded in agreement and wrote "excellent" into her record book. At that moment, I felt vastly superior to my classmates. Perhaps they had not been aware of the subtle irony of my reciting these immortal lines. Had Miss Pfefferkorn understood? I walked home from school with a smile on my face.

III

LEHNITZ

In late spring of 1935, I fell ill with a throat infection. A doctor came to the house to examine me but found nothing wrong with my throat. He told my parents that I was "hysterical" and would soon be better. By early afternoon, however, I had become much worse, and the doctor returned. This time, he looked worried. After a brief conference with my parents, he decided to summon Dr. Else Levy, head of the nose and throat department of the Jewish Hospital of Berlin.

Our dining room was quickly converted into an operating room. Dr. Levy soon arrived on the scene, examined me, and assured my parents that she would be able to help me. A blanket and sheets were placed on the large oak table, a few drops of ether sprinkled onto a handkerchief, and Dr. Levy performed one of those miracles that had earned her the admiration and respect of her colleagues and patients. Skillfully she lanced and drained the large throat abscess that had almost choked me. By evening, I was already feeling much better.

Since I had always been frail, it took me a long time to regain my strength. At the beginning of the school vacation, I was still pale and weak. My parents decided to send me to a children's home in the country, hoping that the fresh air would hasten my convalescence. Only a few recreational places were available to Jewish children. The Jewish Community of Berlin maintained some homes and summer camps near the city. Lehnitz, the home where I was sent, was located northwest of Berlin in a lovely wooded area near the town of Oranienburg. (I did not know then that

Sachsenhausen concentration camp was being built nearby. About 100,000 prisoners would die there.)

I was not yet ten years old and had never been away from home, except for brief stays with relatives. The prospect of going to a place where everybody was Jewish excited me. For the first time in my life, I would not be shunned or ridiculed as an outsider, but I would be accepted as a member of the group.

I was the youngest girl in Lehnitz. Most of the girls in the main building were at least twelve years old, and practically all of them attended private Jewish secondary schools. Our accommodations included a room for every four girls, a communal bathroom and shower on each floor, and a large dining hall downstairs. There were many balconies decorated with flower boxes and a small library we used when rain turned the playing fields into mud. My parents asked one of the supervisors to make sure that I rested several hours each day on one of the balconies, absorbing the sunshine and pure country air. I was not allowed to participate in the prebreakfast runs or strenuous gymnastics that were part of the daily program. I was able to join enough activities, however, to make me feel part of Lehnitz—hikes, song sessions, and, best of all, stimulating discussions.

Each meal began with a spirited Hebrew chorus of *Od lo achalnu* ("we haven't eaten") . . . *yesh lanu teavon* ("we have a [big] appetite")! When the food was brought in, a mighty *beteavon!* ("hearty appetite!") filled the room. And, after the meal, the traditional *Birkat Hamazon* ("Grace after Meals") was sung with the fervor of a revolutionary anthem. The enthusiasm carried me along, and for two weeks I lived in a different world, a world without Hitler salutes, censored books, and blind obedience.

One day, a young rabbi named Max Nussbaum came to talk to us. Speaking with a soft, foreign accent, the Rumanian-born rabbi told us that we Jews should be proud of our heritage. We must return to our ancient homeland, the land that was promised to us. He spoke of the Zionist youth movement whose aim was to reawaken our pride in our common language, Hebrew, and our common history. We must prepare ourselves to become pioneers in Palestine. We must study, train our bodies and our minds. There is no future here, he insisted. Our future is *Eretz Yisrael*.

I had never heard anyone speak so emotionally, yet so perfectly logically; so idealistically, yet so realistically.

Rabbi Nussbaum then joined us in dancing the horah. At first, the circle swayed slowly to the left, but then it gained momentum. Faster and faster it moved, those who tired were pulled along. With a loud *Am Yisrael Chai!* we separated and clapped hands.

On that day I became a Zionist. I resolved then to learn all I could about Judaism, to study Hebrew, to hold my head high. On that day I made a promise that I have kept all my life.

Rabbi Nussbaum returned to Lehnitz several times in those two weeks to lead our discussion groups. The very idea of an intellectual give-and-take was quite new to me. In school, the authority of teacher and principal was never questioned; at home, my father was in control, making all the decisions. We trusted him and believed that he knew best what needed to be done. I can't remember that my sister or I were ever consulted before decisions were made. My mother, naturally, also followed my father's guidance. We must remember that the years of my growing up were, to say the least, unusual. It never occurred to us to doubt our father's wisdom. Every night, when he returned to our small apartment, we were relieved that he had come home safely. There were many children whose fathers were not so fortunate.

In Lehnitz I was exposed, for the first time, to ideas and attitudes that stressed independence. Here we were, sitting in a circle, discussing the pros and cons of kibbutz and city living. Participating in these talks, I learned that your opinions counted even when you were physically dependent on others.

The discussions begun during the day continued into the night. Two of my roommates were students at the Theodor Herzl School, a Jewish day school with a Zionist orientation. These girls did not have to live a dual life. How I envied them their self-confidence!

I do not know to what extent my stay in Lehnitz had strengthened my body. That it had strengthened my spirit, there was no doubt.

When my parents chose Lehnitz, they probably had no idea that they were sending their daughter to a hotbed of Zionism. In those days, Zionism was not yet a household word among the Jews in Germany. In my own family, my father, who had spent many years in France, considered himself a product of the French philosophers. He did not believe that a Jewish state could provide the answers to the problems of the persecuted, wandering Jew. My mother came from a family of assimilated Jews who had played active roles in the Weimar Republic and considered themselves Germans. My grandfather, a respected lawyer, had served for years on the City Council of Koenigsberg. He had such faith in the ultimate power of law and justice that it was impossible for him to foresee the complete disappearance of civilized law. (He was deported to Theresienstadt, where he died at the age of eighty-two.) In the early days of the Hitler regime, many Jews, including rabbis and representatives of the Jewish community, believed that some form of negotiation with the Nazis was possible. Only gradually did Zionism become acceptable and popular.

When Hitler came to power, I was only seven, so I never developed a German Jewish identity. Rabbi Nussbaum had never been a "German" either, and so I could readily identify with him. He gave me hope through the Zionist alternative. In our own land, Jews would not be outcasts.

IV

YELLOW BENCHES

The year 1935 is memorable, not only for my experience in Lehnitz, but also for a number of legal measures that further deprived the German Jews of their civil rights.

When I returned from Lehnitz, I discovered that some of the green wooden benches in the neighborhood park had been painted yellow. On the back was printed, in large black letters, *Nur fuer Juden* ("Only for Jews"). At first I thought it was a stupid joke. How can anyone take such signs seriously? And how silly to waste money, paint, and time on such decorations! But then I realized that this would be just one of the many humiliations the Nazis would dream up. Elderly Jews would huddle on these benches to block the message from view. I made a point of smiling or waving at them—to let them know that I was one of them.

One morning, my cousin Edith phoned. "Marion," she said, in a serious tone, "do you know that on the Olivaer Platz there are *striped* benches?" "Really?" I said. "Yes," said Edith, "they look like zebras. And they are intended for children of mixed marriages." "Are you kidding?" "Yes, I'm kidding," admitted Edith, "but anything is possible. I wonder what they'll think of next!" And then we both laughed.

We didn't have to wait long. Signs began appearing in restaurants and public places: Jews Not Wanted or We Do Not Serve Jews. Some stores, not willing to lose their Jewish customers, would hide these signs behind stacks of dishes or carefully draped curtains. One neighborhood ice-cream parlor, we heard, continued to serve Jews. My sister and I decided to find out for ourselves. We entered the empty shop, and Ulla stepped up to the counter and ordered two portions of ice cream. Then we sat down at a small, round table and watched the clerk arrange the scoops in a glass dish, flanked by two waffles. As the waitress placed the goodies in front of us, my sister called, "Oh, there it is! I see the sign behind the door!" She turned to the startled waitress and said, "I see you won't serve us here!" As the waitress shrugged her shoulders and returned the desserts to the counter, we darted out of the shop without paying.

In September 1935, Germany passed the Nuremberg Laws, depriving Jews of citizenship, the right to vote, and the right to hold public office. To those German Jews who still considered themselves "Jewish Germans," these laws came as a great blow: anti-Semitism had become legal.

The Nuremberg Laws also spelled out the Nazi definition of non-Aryans, that is, Jews. By December 1935, all Jews had been "retired" from the civil service, including public school teachers. At the same time, the quota of Jewish students allowed in the public schools was reduced so drastically that, by April 1936, practically all Jewish children were forced to attend Jewish day schools. With the sudden creation of a large pool of well-qualified teachers and the sudden influx of students of all ages, the existing Jewish schools expanded, and new schools were founded. In addition to the elementary schools (grades 1–8) maintained by the Jewish community, the traditional Orthodox schools, and the Theodor Herzl School, Jewish private schools of every description now appeared.

On the high school level a core curriculum of Jewish studies— Hebrew and Jewish history—was prescribed by the *Reichsvertretung* (a national organization representing German Jews), but the rest of the courses followed, more or less, the standard curriculum of the public school. All schools offered German language and literature, foreign languages, science, history, mathematics, art, music, and physical education. Special schools offered vocational/ commercial training and experimental curricula. Different schools emphasized different subjects and methods of teaching.

After my experience at Lehnitz, I found myself even more isolated in Miss Pfefferkorn's fourth-grade class. I realized that the Nazi doctrine pervaded almost every subject, from literature and science to music and gym. Hitler had begun to "clean up" the German language by removing from the vocabulary all words that had been "borrowed" from other languages. Words like telephone and sauce were replaced by their "pure" German equivalents: *Fernsprecher* and *Tunke*. A dual vocabulary became part of my dual existence. Social studies courses were rewritten to emphasize the virtues of the master race and the inferiority of non-Aryans. Only one subject remained free of ideology: arithmetic. (It is difficult to inject anti-Semitism into the process of long division!) I looked forward to that one hour of nonpropaganda, enjoying the neutrality, logic, and security of the subject.

In April 1936, Miss Pfefferkorn signed my autograph book and wished me well as I left the public school to begin a new life.

V

1936:
A JEWISH SECONDARY SCHOOL
FOR BOYS AND GIRLS

The choice of a Jewish secondary school was not an easy one for my parents. I would have liked to go to the Theodor Herzl School to be among Zionists. But my father could think of many reasons why I should not go there, and, of course, his word was final.

My sister had been attending the public Queen Louise Lycée in Friedenau and had completed the eighth grade. She had been blessed with some rather unusual teachers, some of whom were outspoken anti-Nazis, who had taken a personal interest in her. Ulla had never felt as much an outcast as I. She was a friendly, outgoing girl with a ready smile and a lovely singing voice. In her eleven pre-Hitler years, she had been able to store up some pleasant memories of things German. Ulla and I didn't look like sisters, and our dispositions varied as much as our looks. She was known as "the cheerful Ulla" and I was regarded as the shy and serious one. In 1936, Ulla was a mature fourteen while I was a very immature ten and a half. We had lived separate lives, but, when our father decided to send us both to the same Jewish private school, our relationship changed. Of course, we still had our own circle of friends and different interests, but we now studied in the same school building, attended the same assemblies, and gossiped about the same teachers.

The school was advertised as the "Zickel School, a private, secondary school for boys and girls." It was named for its owner and principal, Miss Luise Zickel, who had founded it about 1909. It was known for its high academic standards and its rigid discipline. The school occupied several floors of a large apartment building on Kufsteiner Street No. 16. Although it lacked a proper gymnasium, locker rooms, and showers, the Zickel School had an excellent physical education program, especially in track and gymnastics. It also provided memorable assemblies, a rigorous academic curriculum, and unforgettable musical activities, both instrumental and vocal. The school attained its maximum size in 1937 when its staff numbered about sixteen and the enrollment topped two hundred. For a short while, we had to be housed in two buildings. After 1937, with stepped-up emigration, the enrollment declined. In the spring of 1939, after an emotional farewell assembly, the school closed.

When I entered the fifth grade at the Zickel School, I didn't know a soul there. My classmate and best friend, Ursel, had moved with her family to another section of Berlin. Ulla had no difficulty adjusting to the new school. She had learned to play the guitar and accompanied herself while singing German and Hebrew songs. A quartet of her classmates met regularly in our apartment: Lotte played the mandolin and Steffi and Ruth sang in harmony. There was always a lot of giggling and whispering. When my mother would enter the room with a plate piled high with sandwiches, I was allowed to join the "big girls." I admired Lotte. She was a member of a Zionist youth organization and, in early 1938, she left for Palestine with the Youth Aliyah. Steffi and Ruth were quiet, gentle girls, very studious and always polite. I believe neither one was able to get out of Germany. After the war, my sister tried to locate them by placing ads in newspapers, but she was unable to trace them. We assume that they perished in the Holocaust.

But, in 1936, when I was beginning my new life at the Zickel School, I truly believed that my dual existence would end. I dreamt of learning without fear and tension. I longed for the atmosphere of Lehnitz.

The apartment house at No. 16 was in the middle of a block of well-kept buildings. It was of utmost importance that the tenants in the neighboring houses not be disturbed by noisy Jewish children. Again we were told not to call attention to ourselves, to remain inconspicuous, lest we stir up anti-Semitism.

Miss Zickel was in complete control of the situation. Although her name (Zickel) means "young goat or kid," there was nothing frisky or playful about her. She was a rotund, middle-aged lady with a firm double chin and thinning gray hair, who always wore long-sleeved, black dresses. Every morning she stationed herself at the top of the stairs, effectively blocking all traffic. The students would climb the stairs in single file, in absolute silence. The girls curtsied quickly as they squeezed by the principal while the boys bowed to her, cap in hand. "Lid off!" she reprimanded those who were struggling with their bookbags and had not yet bared their heads. And, like a carefully rehearsed procession, the girls turned left while the boys continued their climb to the next floor. Miss Zickel saw to it that the boys and girls had separate classrooms in different parts of the building. Snack breaks and recess were scheduled at alternate times so that boy never met girl in the course of the school day. Anyone who strayed into the wrong area was immediately punished, and whoever was foolish enough to be caught dating was suspended.

Once a week, during *Oneg Shabbat,* which was mandated by the Jewish Community of Berlin, boys and girls would share the two adjoining rooms of the first floor "assembly area." Girls would sit on the left and boys on the right, except for the lucky ones who sang in the chorus, played musical instruments, or had parts in a play. I found it difficult to keep my eyes from wandering to the forbidden section of the room. Occasionally a boy would glance over in my direction, and I would feel myself blushing.

One boy, a very shy one, played the violin in most of the assemblies. He never looked at me, but I would watch him intently. (Fourteen years later, in 1950, we married!)

While the atmosphere at the school was a far cry from the egalitarianism of Lehnitz, its rigid structure gave us the illusion of security. The friendships that were formed among the students and between teachers and students were unusually intense. Amid hostile surroundings, the school provided a shelter in which thinking and learning could take place.

VI

SPORTS

The contributions of Germany to the fields of science, medicine, literature, journalism, music, and art are well known. The fact that Jews, as far back as biblical times, engaged in sports, participated in the ancient Olympic Games, and represented their host countries in many international competitions has received less emphasis. In Germany, many Jews were members of the public sports organizations, distinguishing themselves in boxing, swimming, track, gymnastics, fencing, and tennis. All this was to change in 1933. With Hitler's rise to power, all Jewish athletes were expelled from such public sports clubs. Many Jews joined the existing Jewish athletic organizations, notably *Makkabi* (Zionist) and *Schild,* "Shield," (non-Zionist). By 1936 *Makkabi* had 120 affiliated clubs while *Schild* had grown to 126, with a combined total membership of over 40,000. Every imaginable sport was represented, including cycling, mountaineering, and table tennis.

When the *Reichsvertretung* set up the standard curriculum for the Jewish schools, it made physical education a required subject. The Jewish Community of Berlin organized special courses to train teachers as gym instructors. The emphasis on athletics extended even into the Rabbinical Seminary, where participation in sports was mandatory.

I had never enjoyed the gym classes in the German school, where we had to march around for hours in military formation while singing Nazi songs. The one song I remember in particular contained the words *wenn das Judenblut vom Messer spritzt . . .* ("when the Jewish blood spurts off the knife . . ."). I don't think

19

my classmates realized what they were singing. The important thing was to keep the beat and stay in stride. By the time I was ten, I had become an expert marcher.

At the Zickel School I was taught "real" athletics by Miss Portner, a wiry bundle of energy who had absolute control over her body. She tried valiantly to instill in us self-discipline and self-respect. When she left the school to go to England, Miss Ollendorff, the short and stocky French teacher, took her place.

Our small, makeshift gym was equipped with mats, parallel bars, an adjustable horizontal bar, pommel and vaulting horses, springboards, and even a Swedish Ladder (*Sprossenwand*). We all took turns as spotters and mat rollers. The training was rigorous, and each student was expected to master certain basic exercises, according to class level and individual potential. By the time I had reached the seventh grade, I had become a gymnastics enthusiast. My crowning achievement was the handstand on the even parallel bars.

The Jewish Community of Berlin owned a stadium in the Grunewald, a forest preserve southwest of the city. Jewish athletes trained there for the 1936 Olympics. Until November 1938, when the Nazis confiscated the stadium, it was the site of the annual autumn Sportfest in which the Jewish schools competed against each other in track and field.

Every Wednesday, weather permitting, all Zickel students would get off from school at noon, drop off their books at home, have a quick lunch, pick up their gym equipment, and head for the stadium in the Grunewald. The long trip included a trolley ride to the end of the line, followed by a hike through the woods. We would assemble at the trolley terminal and be assigned a partner. It was not considered safe for young girls to walk through the woods alone.

The track at the stadium was covered with coarse cinders. If you fell and scraped your knee, the teacher would paint the wound with iodine. It happened to me quite often, and I remember the smell and the keen sting of the antiseptic. I was a slow runner and no asset on the relay team, but I enjoyed the long jump, high jump, and even the shot put. We also did calisthenics in the center of the field, all the girls of the school in unison, with the teacher in front facing us. I loved the exercise, with the wind in my hair and a sense of belonging in my heart.

After about two hours we would start the trek home. With a little luck, the boys would be leaving the stadium at the same time.

In August 1936, the free world honored Hitler by allowing the Olympic Games to be held in Berlin. Hitler was so eager to have them in Germany that he was willing to make some minor compromises: stores and restaurants removed their We Don't Serve Jews signs for the duration of the event, and Jewish athletes participated in the games. Three Jewish women, representing Hungary, Germany, and Austria, won medals in fencing and received them from the hand of Hitler himself!

My sister, Ulla, and I went back to the ice-cream parlor, paid for our order, and enjoyed every spoonful of it. When the international competitors had left Germany, however, the sign was restored, and we never set foot in the store again.

The success of the Jewish athletes received no notice in the German press, but nobody could hide the fact that Jesse Owens, the black American sprinter, had earned four gold medals. I wondered how Hitler, who fancied himself a member of the super race, must have felt when he faced this "inferior" non-Aryan again and again in the winner's circle. To the Jewish kids of Berlin, Jesse Owens became an instant idol and morale booster. Little did we know that the summer of 1936 was only the calm before the storm. The year 1937 was to see a continuation of Hitler's carefully planned assault on the Jews.

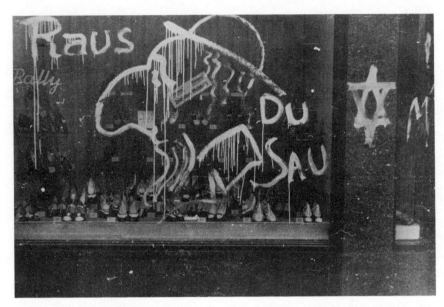

A Jewish-owned shoe store defaced with a paint-smeared star and obscenities, Berlin, November 1938.

Leo Freyer, Marion's father, c. 1948.

Eva Lichtenstein Freyer,
Marion's mother, c. 1948.

Family Pictures:

Marion and Ulla with their grandfather, Dr. Max Lichtenstein, c. 1934.

Hitler opens the 1936 summer Olympics.

Jewish children at a sports festival sponsored by the school system of the Jewish Community of Berlin, 1937.

Prinzregenten Strasse Synagogue, Berlin, designed by Erich Mendelsohn, before and after *Kristallnacht,* 1938.

VII

THE SYNAGOGUE

In Berlin the synagogues were supported through taxation of the Jewish citizens. Whether you attended a synagogue or not, you were obligated to pay the tax. The rabbis were employed by the Jewish Community of Berlin and assigned to a synagogue or rotated from one congregation to another. Only the ultra-Orthodox *Adass Yisroel* group maintained its own schools and synagogues.

Most of the synagogues of Berlin followed the liberal ritual: the service was conducted in Hebrew, the sermon given in German. Some liberal synagogues maintained choirs; most used organs. The Jewish Community of Berlin published a newspaper, the *Gemeindeblatt,* which listed the synagogues, times of services, and the names of the rabbis assigned to officiate on the particular Sabbath or holiday. Some people attended the synagogue, which was located near their homes; others preferred to follow a particular rabbi, no matter where he was assigned.

Because of the system, a rabbi's relationship to the congregation was often distant and formal. The rabbi was the teacher, scholar, interpreter of the texts, and respected leader. After 1933, however, the rabbis were thrust into another role: group therapists to despondent, desperate, and dispossessed Jews, who flocked by the thousands into the synagogues to find consolation and a measure of self-respect. As the Jews of Berlin became progressively ghettoized, the synagogues once again became the meeting places they had been for previous generations. People who had considered themselves emancipated "Jewish Germans" began to realize that this state of equality had been a short-lived illusion. They were reminded daily, through various forms of harassment, that they were non-Aryans and unwelcome in Germany—the country for whom many young Jews had died in the war of 1914–1918. Thus, after 1933, the synagogues were filled to overflowing as the persecuted Jews rediscovered their heritage and found meaning and solace in the ancient chants and prayers that had sustained generations before them.

The last synagogue erected on German soil was a modern structure, designed by the famous architect Erich Mendelsohn. It was located in the Prinzregenten Strasse, within walking distance of our apartment in Friedenau. This synagogue and the dynamic young rabbi who would be assigned to it a few years later would play prominent roles in our life.

The synagogue was a circular building, with a revolving stage, a beautiful organ, and a balcony, which wound around the entire wall. Although it was the first liberal synagogue that allowed women to sit downstairs with the men, I preferred to sit upstairs and see the entire panorama. Shortly after its dedication in the fall of 1930, my mother took Ulla and me to the Prinzregenten Strasse Synagogue for Simchat Torah, traditionally the first holiday service young children attended. The rabbi and the elders of the congregation carried the Torah scrolls, and children of all ages marched behind them, chanting and proudly waving flags. The older children had sewn their own flags, some with elaborate embroidery. These creations were treasured and used year after year. After several circuits, the children walked down the center aisle, were given a few pieces of hard candy, and then rejoined their parents. We walked home in the dark. I insisted that my beautiful, blue velvet flag be fastened to the bedpost to watch over me.

After 1933, every religious service was attended by at least one Gestapo agent. In traditional synagogues, they were easily spotted since they wore no head covering; in Reform congregations, they were less conspicuous. Every rabbi became a ready target of the Gestapo. Fortunately, Berlin was blessed with a number of fearless rabbis who literally put their lives on the line every time they preached a sermon. Dr. Joachim Prinz, an outspoken Zionist, warned the Berlin Jews to expect the worst, but few people heeded his advice. Prinz left Berlin in 1937 for the United States.

Dr. Manfred Swarsensky, ordained in Berlin in 1932 at the age of twenty-six, officiated at the Prinzregenten Strasse Synagogue until the building was burned down in November 1938. Dr. Swarsensky delivered long sermons of almost poetic beauty. His knowledge of history and literature was expansive, and his warmth and wit attracted a large following of young people, not only to the services, but also to his classes.

Dr. Max Nussbaum (whom I had met in Lehnitz) had been ordained in Breslau in 1933. He came to Berlin in 1934 at the age of twenty-four and served the community faithfully until his escape at the end of 1940. He was the last rabbi to leave Berlin for freedom. An eloquent speaker, whose fiery, political sermons drew large crowds of supporters, he was known as the Zionist rabbi. Nussbaum's delivery was unique. When he recited the prayers or blessed the congregation in a deep voice and with that unmistakable, soft Rumanian accent, there was a lyrical, musical quality to his voice. But, when he turned to the daily reality and assailed the British for restricting immigration to Palestine, his voice would ring out, high-pitched and dramatic. On Shavuot 1939, I was one of the thousands who had crowded into the synagogue to hear Dr. Nussbaum talk about the meaning of the holiday. I do not remember what was said about the revelation at Sinai; I do remember what was said about the British White Paper, which effectively ended the legal immigration of Jews into Palestine at the very moment thousands of desperate people sought refuge from Germany.

Other courageous rabbis tried to sustain community morale. I remember in particular Dr. Max Wiener, a soft-spoken scholar and historian. His sermons were not as dramatic as those of Dr.

Nussbaum, nor as literary as those of Dr. Swarsensky. Rather they were lectures on some biblical passage or talmudic text, interpretations of ancient words in the light of modern experience. Much of his message was implied, rather than stated, but the congregation had no difficulty understanding his point. The prophet Habakkuk, for example, in poetry written about 600 B.C., describes the destruction of Judah by the Chaldeans (Neo-Babylonians). The people, assembled in the synagogue in 1939, saw in these ancient words an expression of their very thoughts. Would God answer them as God had Habakkuk?

The most heroic rabbi of all was Dr. Leo Baeck. He chose to remain as leader of the remnant of German Jewry, was deported to Theresienstadt in 1943, miraculously survived, was liberated in 1945, and died in 1956 in London. He has been called "a Saint in Our Time," but he was more than that. To the Berlin Jews he became a symbol of civilized humanity facing bestiality, the father who would not abandon his children, and the fighter who would stand up to the Gestapo, in spite of numerous arrests.

VIII

1937

The year 1937 started badly. My father's factory was seized by the Nazis as the aryanization of Jewish businesses accelerated. The Germans were preparing for war and probably converted to some military purpose the machines that had stamped out buttons and buckles. I have no clear idea of how my father managed to support our family. With characteristic resourcefulness, willpower, and adaptability he found "odd" jobs.

Many Berlin Jews were preparing to emigrate and needed to apply for the required papers. They turned to my father for guidance when the legal tangles became overwhelming. He patiently completed innumerable questionnaires for them, made phone calls, and took their places in the long lines at consulates and steamship offices. I am sure that his quiet diplomacy saved a number of lives. Those who put their trust in him gladly paid for his services. After a long and stressful day, my father would return home late in the evening. He never revealed the nature of his activities. Instead he would read the German classics to us—Goethe and Heine—play chess with me, and help Ulla with her French vocabulary.

Material wealth meant little to my parents. We had always lived frugally. "What you have in your head, nobody can take away from you," my father would say. And his mother had written into my autograph album: "Health and a happy disposition are worth more than money and possessions."

My mother warned me one day that a tax man would come

to look at our furniture. My father had been unable to pay all the taxes, and the government would take furniture in place of cash.

When the tax man arrived, my mother and I greeted him politely. He looked around the small apartment which contained the barest necessities: the large oak dining table, which had served as an operating table in 1935, a couple of bookshelves, one large arm-chair with a cod-liver oil stain dating back to 1922, several straight chairs, two cots in the children's room, and other essential pieces. The tax man looked puzzled. I think he was beginning to feel sorry for us. Perhaps he didn't really want to deprive us of our furniture. At last, he discovered an old chaise longue in my parents' bedroom. "I'll stick the seal here," he said as he pressed a decal with the German eagle on the underside of the daybed. "Next week my colleague will come and take the piece away," he stated as he turned to leave. When he was gone, my mother sighed and said, "We were so lucky! I was afraid he'd take the table. But this old couch needs upholstering anyway, and we won't miss it." It then occurred to me that the piano had vanished some time ago. I surmised that an eagle had been stuck on it, too, but we didn't talk about it. After all, Ulla was now playing the guitar and seemed to enjoy that more than practicing the piano.

It was about that time that my mother began to ask me occasion-ally to stop for dinner at the day-care center maintained by the Jewish Community of Berlin. In Europe it is customary to eat the main meal in the middle of the day, at one or two o'clock, and have a light supper in the evening. School began at 8:00 A.M. and ended at about 1:30 P.M. Students ate dinner at home, and some returned to school for recorder lessons, crafts classes, or work in the library before settling down for hours of homework.

Whenever my mother gave me a few coins for a meal, I would sign in at the Jewish day-care center. None of my classmates from the Zickel School had ever gone there. "The regulars" were a rough and noisy bunch of kids who eyed me, a shy stranger, with suspicion. The counselor assigned seats around a very long table, and then the food was rolled in on steel carts. I remember three main dishes: warm potato salad, Spanish rice, and a thick bean soup. The counselor filled each plate, which the children passed along until everyone was served. There were no appetizers and no desserts, only heaps of potato salad or tomato rice. Before digging in, we all chanted the appropriate blessings. It was filling fare, and we were allowed to have seconds. Then, just as at Lehnitz, we chanted the "Grace after Meals" with enthusiasm. When I joined the singing and drummed on the table to emphasize the important words, I became one with the group. "Rebuild Jerusalem speedily in our days!" we shouted in Hebrew. I felt accepted.

A spiritual high point of an otherwise bad year was Ulla's confirmation at the Prinzregenten Strasse Synagogue. Ulla was thirteen or fourteen when she began attending Dr. Swarsensky's classes on the Hebrew prophets. The message of the prophets, their emphasis on righteousness, justice, and humility, made a deep impression on my sister. While we were surrounded by hate and brutality, Dr. Swarsensky taught that love and kindness are the essence of Judaism, and concern for all people is our sacred obligation. When Ulla later chose a career in social work, particularly in caring for former mental patients, she applied the values and precepts emphasized by Rabbi Swarsensky.

That May 1937, during the Shavuot services, Ulla sat on the synagogue stage as a member of the confirmation class. In those days it was not customary for girls to celebrate Bat Mitzvah, and very few continued their studies to age fifteen or beyond to be confirmed. During the holiday of Shavuot, commemorating the giving of the Ten Commandments on Mount Sinai and celebrating the first harvest in ancient and modern Israel, the Ten Commandments are read during the service. It was only natural that ten of the confirmands offered explanations and interpretations of the Decalogue, leaving two girls without a commandment of their own. The rabbi had arranged that one of them would deliver a short introductory speech and Ulla would conclude the ceremony with a poem.

I do not recall what dress my sister wore, nor whether Dr. Swarsensky delivered a sermon. I do remember every word of the poem, however, and, when I visited Rabbi Swarsensky in Madison, Wisconsin, thirty-three years later, I recited it for him. It began:

Das sind nicht wir,
Das ist das Judentum worum es geht
Im Kampfe aller Rassen.
Das sind nicht wir,
Das ist das Heiligtum um das es geht,
Um Liebe oder Hassen.
Das sind nicht wir,
Denn dieser Kampf waer Nichts,
Wenn es um Menschen geht
Die sterblich sind.
Es geht um die Idee des Ewigen Lichts,
Mit dem Es endet, mit dem Es beginnt. . . .

The meaning of the poem, which appears in its entirety at the end of this book, may be summarized as follows: The aim of the struggle in which Jews find themselves in these days is *not* to preserve the lives of individuals but, rather, to save Judaism itself. Each human being is likened to a flickering candle, easily extinguished. It is the idea of the Eternal Light that we are struggling to preserve. It is the fight between love and hate, light and darkness, the Holy and the profane. We have been chosen to conduct this fight, and our life is one of suffering. A mark of pain is etched into our faces. And, while the tears may flow, pride silences all complaints.

(The author of this poem is not known to me.)

I also recall that this service was the last one my father attended in Germany. During the Hitler years, he avoided any activity that would mark him as a Jew. As a child, I regretted his lack of involvement, and I saw in it a lack of support for my own struggle to achieve an identity. As I grew older, I realized that his desire for anonymity was his way of "not calling attention to oneself." He never affiliated with any group—religious, cultural, or political—and his name never appeared on any membership list. He is convinced that this anonymity saved his life in the pogrom of November 1938, and he may well be right.

The rabbi concluded the service with the Priestly Blessing:

> May the Lord bless thee and keep thee;
> May the Lord make His countenance to shine upon thee
>   and be gracious unto thee;
> May the Lord turn His countenance unto thee and give
>   thee peace.

My parents had given Ulla a portable, hand-wound victrola and two or three classical records. I had carefully leaked this information to all relatives and friends who had been invited. When they appeared in the afternoon to join us for "coffee" and cake, each one carried a record—a Haydn symphony, several Chopin and Liszt piano pieces, some operatic arias, and one strange record called "I've Got a Feelin' You're Foolin'," sung by Eleanor Powell, an American musical comedy star. My sister cranked up the victrola (it had to be rewound for each record), put the record on the turntable, and put her ear to the sound box. A hush fell over the guests as we strained to catch the meaning of the foreign words. We realized how little our English lessons had prepared us for a popular American song. Midway in the record, the music stopped and the sound of horses' hooves took over. "There's a flaw in this record," said Ulla, examining the disc for a scratch. After a little while, the music picked up again, only to be followed by another interlude of syncopated horse patter. Cousin Hans Peter came to the rescue. "What you hear is called tap dancing," he explained. "That's how they dance in America, and Eleanor Powell is very good at it." "I can't make out the words," said my mother, "she sings in such a nasal way." Cousin Hans Peter smiled. "In America, that's called sexy," he said.

IX

CULTURE

Imagine waking one morning to find that newspaper columnists
Ann Landers and Art Buchwald are no longer allowed to pub-
lish; cartoonist Herblock has been dismissed; movies featuring
Charlie Chaplin, Woody Allen, Danny Kaye, the Marx Brothers,
or Barbra Streisand are forbidden. Pinchas Zukerman, Isaac Stern,
Yitzhak Perlman, Artur Rubinstein, and André Previn are barred
from the stage and the recordings of these "degenerates and racial
undesirables" destroyed. Imagine "God Bless America" by Irving
Berlin, *Porgy and Bess* by Ira and George Gershwin, *West Side
Story* by Leonard Bernstein, *A Lincoln Portrait* by Aaron Copland
officially censored as anti-American. Imagine also all Jewish medical scientists—Jonas Salk (polio), Albert Sabin (polio), Steven Ro-
senberg (cancer), and hundreds of researchers at the National
Institutes of Health—forced to retire.

Imagine all books written by Jewish authors removed from
the libraries and burned, along with paintings by Jewish artists.
Picture a society where the works not only of Jews but also of
"philo-Semitic" non-Jews (like Thomas Mann) are banned, where
some Mozart operas can no longer be staged because the libretti
were written by a half-Jew, Lorenzo da Ponte, and where Handel's
Judas Maccabaeus is performed under a different title and with
a different text. No film directed by a Jew can be shown; no
play produced by a Jew can be performed; no song written by a
Jew can be sung. The radio and television are "cleansed" of Jewish
voices and faces, and all Jewish actors and musicians are dismissed.

That it is possible for such a society to exist, there is no doubt.

Neither is there any doubt that the level of culture, of civilization, and of humanity of such a society would be drastically reduced. Now try to imagine that the void, created when the products of Jewish minds were banned, is filled with pagan symbols, vicious propaganda, and constantly repeated lies, and you have a picture of Germany during the years 1933–1945. In two or three years the progress of hundreds of years had been wiped out.

The Jewish Community of Berlin was blessed with men and women of extraordinary organizational ability, vision, and courage. It was these devoted leaders who created and maintained the social, educational, and cultural institutions, enabling the Berlin Jews to survive and function under the most difficult circumstances. Every Friday night, when the rabbis led their congregations in a special prayer for the health and safety of the leading officers of the Jewish community, its representatives, teachers, and "all those who devote themselves to the welfare of the community," I would think especially of my "heroes," the rabbis and the leaders of the *Kulturbund,* the Jewish Cultural Association, created to provide employment for thousands of artists, who had suddenly become jobless.

The moving spirit, cofounder (with theater critic Julius Bab), and head of the *Kulturbund* was Dr. Kurt Singer. A neurologist by profession, and the conductor of the "Doctors' Choir" by avocation, he had been appointed in 1927 to head the Municipal Opera House of Berlin. On April 1, 1933 (the day of the boycott against Jewish businesses), Dr. Singer and a committee of Jewish experts drew up a proposal for a Jewish Cultural Association. He then presented the plans to the German authorities and, on June 16, 1933, was granted permission for the establishment of the *Kulturbund,* "a permanent theater by Jews and for Jews, alternating operas and dramas, and encompassing the world repertoire as well as Jewish themes." For some strange reason, the authorities seemed to support only two movements among German Jewry: emigration and the *Kulturbund.* Later, in the concentration camps, the Nazis permitted, even forced, artists to perform until they were put to death. Perhaps the Nazis saw in the *Kulturbund* a similar, twisted link between art and death.

Dr. Singer's task was to build an organization able to maintain, exclusively through Jewish labor and membership, two permanent troupes, one for operas and the other for plays. Workshops were set up to sew the costumes and build the scenery. Monthly membership fees were set at two and a half marks, for which members were offered two presentations, alternating between operas and lectures, plays and concerts. The organization was joined by 19,000 people; 200 persons were given steady employment. Moreover, as a social organization, the *Kulturbund* helped the Jews cope with their increasing isolation and loneliness. It also functioned as an educational vehicle to help the German Jews rediscover their Jewishness. Gradually a repertoire evolved that pleased the Zionists as well as the more German-oriented members of the community.

Operas by Mozart, Verdi, Puccini, Rossini, and others were performed. Wagner, Lortzing, and Weber, "for reasons of tact," were not represented. As time went on, the orchestras in Berlin and in the provinces lost more and more members to emigration. There was such an acute shortage of wind instruments that it became difficult to perform symphonic music. Choirs, however, flourished in all the small and large towns, providing not only music but much-needed fellowship.

The choice of plays also presented problems, but a repertoire including classical as well as "Jewish" plays was developed through the years. Stefan Zweig's *Jeremias*, performed in 1934, was a huge success, as were plays translated from Yiddish and Hebrew. Jewish playwrights whose works were banned on the German stage found a warm welcome in the *Kulturbund*, side by side with Shakespeare, Goethe, Lessing, Shaw, Molière, Tolstoy, Ibsen, and Sophocles.

The *Kulturbund* also maintained a "Theater for Youth," which performed occasional matinees in cooperation with the Jewish schools. In addition, it sponsored exhibitions by painters and sculptors and a lecture series. Jewish writers and poets were given an opportunity to read from their works. In 1937, a prize competition was organized to stimulate the creation of contemporary Jewish music. That year there were 60,000 members in one hundred towns throughout Germany. Between October 1933 and October 1938, a total of 8,457 presentations were given by the affiliated Jewish cultural organizations. The *Kulturbund* had become a symbol for spiritual resistance.

Even after the destruction of the synagogues on November 9, 1938, the Gestapo insisted that the *Kulturbund* continue its activities. Amid the smoldering temples and ransacked businesses, the Jewish theater remained untouched. Some of the staff members had been arrested but were released within a few days so that the shows could go on. The plays continued into 1940, carefully supervised by three Gestapo agents who attended every performance and were easily identified by their bowler hats and briefcases. Their job was to make sure that only plays approved by the authorities were performed and that the actors stuck to their lines.

Dr. Singer died in 1944 in Theresienstadt at age fifty-nine. Many others who had been active in the *Kulturbund* perished in Auschwitz.

As a child I was very much aware of the existence of the *Kulturbund,* even though I was always told that I was too young to attend any of the performances. John (my future husband) was exactly my age, and his parents considered him old enough to attend! He counts the hours he spent at the Jewish theater among the happiest memories of his youth. Ulla occasionally attended performances when friends offered her their tickets. She would come home, glowing with excitement, and tell me all about the opera, play, or lecture she had attended. Sometimes we would read the play she had just seen, and, in this way, I also benefited. Looking back, I believe that it was our lack of money, and my father's desire for anonymity, rather than my age, that prevented us from buying a subscription to the series.

In 1937, the Zickel School occupied a "real" school building in the Schmargendorfer Street to accommodate the large influx of students. (In the summer of 1938, the school moved back into the apartment building on Kufsteiner Street.) It had a gymnasium with a stage and curtains. Dr. Gertrud Landsberg, our dynamic music teacher, decided to take advantage of these facilities by preparing a production of Mozart's *The Magic Flute,* an ambitious undertaking involving the entire school. Landsie, as everyone called her, had adapted the opera to the resources at hand: a small stage, children's voices, and one piano, played by André Previn, then eight years old and a student at the Zickel School. Landsie condensed the opera to about one-third its length, retaining the lovely, familiar tunes but eliminating the recitatives. She rewrote the orchestral parts for a recorder ensemble and piano accompaniment. We spent months listening to records, painting scenery, sewing costumes, and rehearsing the arias and choral numbers. "In these holy halls revenge is unknown" the students' chorus was singing earnestly while nearby the German authorities were laying the plans for our destruction.

X

CHANGES

When my parents got married in 1920, at the height of the German inflation, apartments were almost impossible to find. They considered themselves lucky when they discovered a two-bedroom place in a corner house in Friedenau. Our family lived there until the fall of 1937 when the 150-year-old apartment house was demolished. It was no great loss! The building was overrun with roaches and other creepy creatures that resided in layers of wallpaper. Even periodic fumigating had little effect. Occasionally hungry little mice invaded our quarters. Our apartment was so drafty that my mother put layers of newspapers underneath the worn rugs to keep the heat in.

In each room there was a tiled furnace. The coal to heat it was delivered in flat, wooden boxes containing exactly 100 briquettes, each weighing 500 grams. Since coal was expensive, we used it sparingly and efficiently. My father had calculated the exact number of pieces of coal we could afford to use each day. Many chilly days I would bundle up in blankets, and, before going to bed, I would warm up the sheets with a flat, shiny stone from the tile oven. In the morning, at the sound of the alarm, I'd hop out of bed into the cold air and build a fire in the tiled furnace of the room I shared with Ulla. It was fun to arrange four briquettes of soft coal on top of a few slivers of kindling wood and crumpled paper, throw a match in, and stand back to admire the roaring flames. I had become quite adept at this ritual and felt proud that my parents trusted me with fire.

When the authorities decided that the entire block was to be razed to make room for the Zeiss Optical Company, signs were

posted on the houses marked for demolition. They read Thank
Your *Fuehrer* ("leader") and Hitler Builds. My father explained
that Zeiss was building a factory there to produce precision instruments for German submarines. So it was Hitler's armament program that was the immediate cause of our moving to another
neighborhood.

We were fortunate to find a two-bedroom apartment in a nice
area within walking distance of the Zickel School. The apartment
was located on the ground level of a "rear" building on Barbarossa
Street. The "front" building, through which one had to pass to
reach the "garden houses" (as the rear buildings were called),
had a large lobby with velvety rugs, an elevator, and large glass
doors with iron bars. There were no rugs or elevators in the
rear buildings, but we didn't care. Our new home had hot running
water and central heating. What luxury! I wouldn't need to build
any more fires in the morning. After the furniture had been arranged
according to my mother's directions, my father surveyed our new
home and announced sarcastically, "We thank our *Fuehrer* for
this."

After my father lost his business, he found it more and more
difficult to pay our tuition costs. Miss Zickel customarily handed
statements in white envelopes to those whose payments were up
to date and blue envelopes to those whose payments were overdue.
I received blue envelopes quite regularly. My classmates would
giggle when they would see me singled out—the kid with a letter
of a different color. After we had moved to Barbarossa Street,
where rents were higher than in Friedenau, my father fell even
further behind in the tuition payments.

The Jewish Community of Berlin maintained a variety of helping
agencies for people impoverished by Hitler's policies. One office,
called "Parents' Aid" (*Elternhilfe*), provided scholarships for good
students. In 1937, I became a scholarship student, and I had to
report regularly, in person, to my social worker, Miss Zwirn,
about my grades and activities. Miss Zwirn, a warm and supportive
lady, decided whether my scholarship would be renewed.

In the fall of 1937, Miss Zickel placed an advertisement with a British scholastic agency, asking for two qualified teachers to give English lessons in her school. In those days there was widespread unemployment among teachers in England, and a number of candidates applied. Miss Zickel chose Mr. Dobson for the boys and Miss Riley for the girls. The terms of employment included room and board plus salary.

There was no lack of motivation to learn English. Young and old signed up for classes in Hebrew and English to prepare for life overseas. Mr. Dobson taught classes during school hours, after school, and in the evening. Many of his pupils at night were professional men—doctors and lawyers—who required quick improvement of their English for emigration.

Miss Zickel informed the parents of her students that English classes would be available for an additional fee. Of course, my father wanted me to learn English, but he saw no way to come up with more money. Miss Zickel decided to exclude me (and Vera, another scholarship student) from the English classes. When the other girls filed into their classroom to absorb Miss Riley's perfect accents, Vera and I would go to the library and try to look unconcerned. On field days, the girls would cluster around Miss Riley, a very popular, vivacious blonde, and chatter with her. Since Miss Zickel had ordained that the English teachers were to be addressed in English only, I couldn't join the conversation. How far can one get on "How do you do?" and a shy smile?

I was an outsider again. In the German school, I had been shunned because I was Jewish; in the Jewish school, I was made to feel different because I was poor.

When the time came to report to Miss Zwirn, my father suggested that I discuss the matter with her. Miss Zwirn was outraged that Vera and I were denied English lessons. "I will see to it that you will learn English," she said, "but not at the Zickel School!" A few days later, Vera and I began our lessons with a retired schoolteacher who was delighted to welcome us into her home two afternoons per week after school. I wish I could recall the tutor's name! She was an excellent teacher, patient but demanding. On cold days, she would have cookies and hot tea for us, "for educational purposes," she would say. She tried to show us how to balance cup, cookie, and napkin daintily on our laps, "as they do at English tea parties." I often think of my gentle tutor with gratitude. My command of English has improved considerably, but, when it comes to the balancing act, I am still a total failure.

XI

EMIGRATION

Hitler's program for the total destruction of the Jews proceeded on schedule. In the first phase, 1933–1936, Jews were excluded from the rest of German society—politically, socially, and economically. During the second phase, 1937–1939, the emphasis was on the expropriation and expulsion of the Jews from Germany. During the third phase, 1939–1945, came the "Final Solution," the mass murder of the remaining Jews. Hitler successfully executed his plan in broad daylight as the world stood by in silent inaction.

On March 13, 1938, Hitler annexed Austria without resistance. In fact, the Austrians welcomed the Germans more as liberators than conquerors. All the anti-Jewish legislation, which had been passed in Germany in five years, immediately went into effect in Austria. The Viennese Jews were subjected to such terrible humiliations, sadism, and murders that many resorted to suicide. Many fled in panic to Switzerland, Italy, and Czechoslovakia, until those countries closed their borders.

At the Munich Conference in September 1938, France, England, and Italy, in an effort to avoid another world war, surrendered to Hitler the Sudetenland, a German-speaking part of Czechoslovakia. Emboldened by this show of weakness, and in violation of the agreement they had made, the Nazis occupied all of Czechoslovakia in March 1939.

Meanwhile, the impoverishment of the German Jews continued. In April 1938, a decree was passed requiring the registration of all Jewish wealth exceeding 5,000 marks ($2,000). Jews had to deposit their money in certain banks and were told how much they were allowed to withdraw. In July 1938, all Jewish physicians lost their licenses to practice. Two months later, all Jewish lawyers were disbarred. Business licenses of salesmen and agents were withdrawn. The synagogues of Munich, Nuremberg, and Düsseldorf were destroyed in a "slum clearance" operation. In June 1938, the Nazis began making mass arrests of Berlin Jews on the pretext that they had criminal records. For many the charge was based on minor traffic violations. Those arrested were imprisoned in the Sachsenhausen concentration camp and had to flee the country upon their release. At the same time, raids of Jewish homes became more frequent. Gestapo agents would search homes for forbidden books, claim "evidence" of illegal activities, and arrest innocent people on trumped-up charges.

In August 1938, a law was passed forcing Jews to change their names. It stipulated that, effective January 1, 1939, all Jewish males had to adopt "Israel" and all Jewish females "Sara" as their middle names. If your name happened to be Solomon, Itzig, or Feigele, you were exempt. If the last name contained any reference to Germany, the bearer was to change it "voluntarily" to the maiden name of one of the grandmothers. The family of Inge Deutschkron was ordered to change its surname because it meant "German crown."

In October 1938, a law was passed requiring the red letter *J* (*Jude*, "Jew") on Jewish passports. During the same month about 17,000 Polish Jews, who for many years had lived in Germany, were deported to Poland under inhuman conditions. They wandered around for days along the Polish border before their native land agreed to admit them.

Life was becoming more difficult from day to day, and everybody had one thought in mind: **emigration.**

According to Webster, emigration is "the act of leaving one country or region to settle in another." This simple definition gives no hint of the requirements of emigration in the modern world. For every act of leaving, two conditions need to be met: first, the country of residence must give permission to leave, and, second, the receiving country must permit entry. Satisfaction of one requirement in no way guarantees satisfaction of the other.

In October 1938, the Jewish Book Publishing Company in Berlin published the *Philo Atlas: Handbuch fuer die juedische Auswanderung* ("Handbook for the Jewish Emigration"). This little volume immediately became a best-seller of sorts. Practically every Jewish family owned the *Philo Lexicon* and the *Philo Atlas,* two indispensable reference books. The following definition appeared on page 11 of the *Philo Atlas:*

> Emigration means . . . a complete alteration of all the customary conditions of life: climate and nutrition, language and customs; professional expectations and political circumstances are in the country of immigration, even within Europe, totally different from what one is used to. Therefore, emigration makes tremendous demands on physical, mental, and emotional adaptability. In general only young people are fully capable of such adjustments.

The author of the *Philo Atlas* then lists the four most important "Commandments of Emigration":

1. Planning ahead: Gather information concerning all the opportunities and difficulties of the country of immigration.

2. Willingness to accept any type of work. Ordinarily the immigrant must begin again in a status much below his present one. "There is nothing humiliating about this" (the author of the *Philo Atlas* adds consolingly).

3. Intensive effort must be made to master the new language.

4. The immigrant must be willing to relocate from large cities to smaller towns, which are less overrun by émigrés.
   Only under such conditions will emigration, especially to countries overseas, lead to success.

Faced with such demands, it is no wonder that many German Jews, especially those who were successful in their professions, hesitated for years to initiate the process of emigration.

Leaders of the Jewish community tried to encourage people to prepare for emigration. Language classes were set up and eagerly attended. Since some countries gave preference for admission to manual workers and agricultural laborers, an extensive and intensive retraining program was organized. Lawyers trained to become shoemakers; women took up dressmaking; doctors became carpenters. The Zionist organization set up training camps to prepare young people for work in agriculture.

It was up to the individual to take the first steps towards emigration, mainly to find relatives abroad who would agree to serve as sponsors. Once the decision was made, a network of Jewish aid organizations provided assistance in the actual process. The rabbis tried to maintain the morale of those who were near despair. The problem of emigration was not new to the Jewish people, they said. Had not Jeremiah urged the people to leave Jerusalem? The Jewish people, a people of wanderers, a people of God, will survive. We will carry our heritage with us no matter where we will be scattered. One Friday night in early 1938, in place of a sermon, Rabbi Swarsensky recited these stirring lines from Stefan Zweig's 1917 drama *Jeremias:*

Wandervolk, Gottesvolk,	People of wanderers, peo-
hebe dich auf!	ple of God, arise!
Lasset die Toten,	Leave the dead,
Sie haben den Frieden,	They have their peace,
Lasset die Mauern,	Leave the walls,
Sie stehen nicht auf,	They will not rise,
Du doch erstehest	But you arise
Ewig und ewig,	Eternally,
Aus deinen Tiefen	Out of your depths
In deinem Gott.	In your God.
Auf,	Arise,
Wandervolk, Gottesvolk,	People of wanderers, peo-
rüste zur Reise,	ple of God, prepare for
	the journey,

Blick in die Ferne,	Look to the distance,
Blick nicht zurück!	Do not glance back!
Die verweilen,	Those who remain
Haben die Heimat,	Have the homeland,
Doch die wandern,	But those who wander
Haben die Welt!	Have the world!
Auf, ihr Gebeugten,	Arise, you who are bowed down,
Auf, ihr Besiegten,	Arise, you who have been conquered,
Gott hat die Straßen,	The roads you are traveling
Die ihr beschreitet,	God has prepared them
Wissend bereitet,	knowingly,
Wandervolk, Gottesvolk,	People of wanderers, peo-
auf in die Welt!	ple of God, go forth into the world!

In 1933, approximately 525,000 Jews lived in Germany. Nearly 60 percent emigrated; but, of those that found refuge in other European countries, about 30,000 perished in the Holocaust. The first deportations (Baden, Stettin, Vienna, Prague, Moravska-Ostrava) began in early 1940. On October 1, 1941, legal emigration from Germany came to an end. At the end of the war, about 10,000 Jews (5,000 in hiding and 5,000 returnees from concentration camps) had survived in Germany.

For the Jewish Community of Berlin, the following figures were published in 1987 in the *Wegweiser durch das juedische Berlin:*

Jewish population of Berlin, 1933: about 160,000 (census of June 16, 1933: 160,564)

By 1945: about
    90,000 had emigrated
    55,000 had been murdered in concentration camps
     7,000 had died, most by suicide

Of the surviving 8,000 Jews: about
    4,700 had non-Jewish spouses
    1,900 returned from concentration camps
    1,400 survived in hiding

XII

THE NUMBERS GAME

S oon after Hitler's rise to power, my father realized that, eventually, we would have to leave Germany. He had visited Holland in 1934 and France in 1936 to see if he could establish a new existence for us there. But his observations convinced him that the European continent could not provide the necessary economic opportunities. "We must get out of Europe," he said. "We have no future here."

So, in 1937, my father began his search to locate our American relatives. His father had been the youngest of eleven siblings, eight girls and three boys. The four oldest sisters had left Germany about 1870. At that time, under Bismarck, Jews had been granted full German citizenship, including the obligation to serve in the German army. Many Jewish families sailed for America to avoid the draft. The four sisters maintained their ties with the family, and my father recalls that Aunt Friederike and her husband visited in 1895–1896, and Aunt Esther and her husband and son visited in 1901. My father, then eight years old, lived in Lyck, a small town in what was then East Prussia, near the Russian border. Another relative came from America at the time of my father's Bar Mitzvah in 1906.

By 1933, the older relatives were no longer alive, and the young generation, born in America, failed to maintain family ties. My father asked the National Council of Jewish Women in the United States to assist him in contacting our American relatives. It was vital that these family members be located so that we could get on the waiting list for an American quota number, the golden key to the New World.

America restricted the number of immigrants through a quota system. In 1921, Congress had passed a quota law, limiting the number of immigrants from a given European country to 3 percent of the nationality's population residing in the United States in 1910. In 1924, the quotas were reduced to 2 percent, based on the earlier 1890 United States census. Amendments were passed in 1929 fixing the annual quota at about 150,000. The quota system effectively reduced emigration from southern and eastern Europe while favoring the northern countries. Great Britain and Ireland were assigned about 83,000 places, which were never used, while Germany was allotted about 27,000. Poland, with a Jewish population of over three million, had only 6,000 quota places. American consuls in Europe were given the task of assigning quota numbers and visas. Unfortunately, the discretionary power to exclude those "likely to become a public charge" was used by some consuls to reject applicants on the basis of personal prejudice and rigid conformity.

Some groups were admitted to the United States outside the regular quota: rabbis who had been offered jobs by American congregations; scholars and college professors who had been guaranteed positions; and renowned scientists, including ten Nobel Prize winners in physics—Albert Einstein, Niels Bohr, and Enrico Fermi among them. After 1940, the International Rescue Committee, under the leadership of Varian Fry, managed to save about 1,500 well-known scholars, scientists, artists, and religious and labor leaders by forging papers and establishing escape routes—via Spain, to Portugal, and from the port of Lisbon to the United States.

These daring rescue efforts, however, were the exceptions. Even after it became known that the Jews of Europe were being annihilated, neither Congress nor President Roosevelt made any effort to relax the rigid quota system. As a result, my father's mother and sister, my mother's father and sister, and many other relatives and friends, all of whom held affidavits and had been placed on waiting lists for quota spaces, were condemned to die in extermination camps. Jews did want to emigrate, but no country would accept them. America with its quota system and England, which denied the Jews entry into Palestine, bear a great burden of guilt.

The ladies of the National Council of Jewish Women managed to locate members of my father's family, and we began exchanging letters and photos with my father's cousins. With his German-English dictionary in hand, my father tried to explain our dire predicament. We needed affidavits for four people in order to get our names on the waiting list for quota numbers. An affidavit is a sworn statement of a sponsor guaranteeing financial responsibility for a prospective immigrant. A sponsor had to leave a sizable deposit in the bank, as proof that resources were available, to ensure against the immigrant's becoming a burden to the state. One of the relatives was economically able to help us; others wrote us that they had lost their savings during the depression and were struggling themselves.

We were overjoyed to learn that one of the cousins had agreed to sponsor us and believed that we might be able to get out within a year. My father went to the American consulate and showed the notarized documents his cousin had sent him. Alas, the cousin was born in 1872 and, since he had just turned sixty-six, was judged to be too old to be our sole sponsor. Another, younger, relative needed to be found who would act as co-sponsor. Carlos, the grandson of Aunt Esther, volunteered to save us.

At last, on November 28, 1938, we received notification from the American consulate that we had been put on a waiting list for the German quota. It was a significant step forward but certainly no guarantee that our number would be called in time for us to get out of Germany. The nerve-racking wait would last almost another year.

Leo Baeck, rabbi of the Jewish Community of Berlin, 1912–1943, became the spiritual leader of German Jewry as a whole after the Nazi seizure of power in 1933.

A concert, one of 600 presented by the *Kulturbund* during the Nazi years, at the Oranienburger Strasse Synagogue, Berlin, 1938.

Ruins of the Fasanen Strasse Synagogue, *Kristallnacht,* 1938.

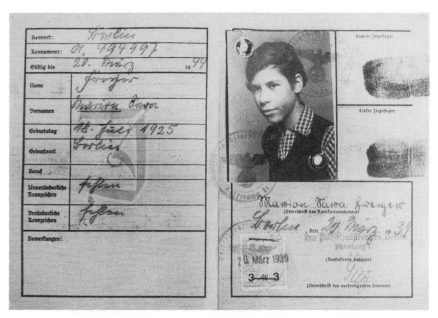

Marion Freyer's *Kennkarte* with the registration number, a photo showing the left ear of its bearer, and the middle name "Sara," which was added to the names of Jewish females to identify them as Jews, March 20, 1939.

Dr. Gertrud Landsberg, music teacher at the Zickel School, 1939.

Hans Bruno Wolff, age 13,
and his sister Marianne, age 10,
Berlin, summer 1938.

XIII

LIFE GOES ON

Against a background of more restrictions, more poverty, and more insecurity, Ulla and I, nevertheless, lived the first ten months of 1938 to the fullest. The Jewish schools, which had sprung up by necessity, were small enough for everyone to get to know one's classmates. For many, the schools provided the love and stability of an extended family.

In 1938, emigration had become the overriding preoccupation of home and school. Every student was preparing for life outside of Germany. We assumed that emigration would be possible for all of us. In school, each subject took on the importance of a "survival skill": English, French, and Hebrew were vital, as were geography and history. Geography, taught by Dr. Martin Warschauer, became a major subject. We painstakingly copied detailed maps of the United States, Palestine, England, and France. We studied the city maps of New York and London. Every seventh grader at the Zickel School was able to locate Central Park and the Brooklyn Bridge on a map. Dr. Kate Laserstein, who taught us German grammar and literature, suspected that we might never study those subjects again. She had us memorize many of the classical poems and parts of plays. "Whatever you have in your head, nobody can take away from you," I was told at home and at school. In physical education, the disciplines of gymnastics, calisthenics, and track strengthened our bodies and our self-control. Team sports received little emphasis.

But it was in our music classes with Dr. Gertrud Landsberg (Landsie) that we learned our most important lessons—music is a universal idiom that bridges all languages and all cultures. We sang: "All that is earthbound must eventually decay. Music, however, will eternally stay." (*Alles was irdisch muss endlich vergehn. Musika bleibet in Ewigkeit stehn.*) The dual gymnasium-music room became a refuge from the dangers and uncertainties outside. Through music we transcended the quest for affidavits and quota numbers. Every night, while doing the dishes, Ulla and I would sing canons together, forging a lasting bond between us.

As I was a scholarship student, I felt a special urgency to perform well in all subjects. But I loved to study, and my reading, especially in the Jewish subjects, far exceeded the requirements. I tutored my less diligent classmates for a fee of half a mark per lesson, which I spent on caramel candies, still easily obtainable, but ruinous to my teeth.

There was more to our life than school. For family get-togethers and birthday parties, my mother would write humorous skits, which Ulla and I performed. Young and old played word games, sang together, exchanged foreign stamps. Even though food was scarce, we occasionally invited friends to share our meals, often noodles with applesauce or potato pancakes. "F.H.B.," my mother would warn us—"family holds back" until the guests had enough to eat. And, after the meal, my father would read the hilarious satires of the Swedish humorist, Hasse Zetterstroem, and everyone would leave laughing.

In April 1938, Ulla graduated from the Zickel School. Jews were not permitted to attend the university, and so Ulla continued her education at the business college maintained by the Jewish Community of Berlin. She studied typing and shorthand (both in German and English), commercial geography, English language, and business correspondence. Soon she developed such speed in English shorthand that she began giving lessons to a number of experienced, middle-aged secretaries who were preparing for emigration.

In July 1938, my mother and I traveled by train to Koenigsberg to spend the school vacation at my grandfather's home. My grandmother had died three years earlier, and my Aunt Kate kept house for my grandfather. Koenigsberg, a picturesque, old city on the river Pregel in East Prussia, had an active Jewish community of about 2,600. Its numerous Zionist activists had left for Palestine in the early thirties. The remaining families all knew each other, and most of the youngsters were members of Bar Kochba, a Jewish sports club. That summer of 1938, I spent most of my time with the Bar Kochba group on the athletic field, located adjacent to the Jewish cemetery. Hannelore, a girl of my age whom I had met on earlier trips to Koenigsberg, greeted me at the trolley stop and introduced me to her friends on the playing field. She was an ardent Zionist and told me that her sister had left for Palestine with the Youth Aliyah and that she was planning to follow her as soon as she reached fourteen. Her older brother, Fritz, remained in Koenigsberg with their parents.

Mr. Weinberg, the gym teacher at the Jewish school, was in charge of the daily activities. In the morning, the girls would gather around the portable organ at one corner of the lawn while Mr. Weinberg played the theme from Schumann's Fourth Symphony. We had worked out a precise, rhythmic calisthenics routine, which we performed in time with the music. The boys, meanwhile, practiced shot put at the other end of the field. All other activities were co-ed. Mr. Weinberg was a relaxed and good-natured coach who had invented a race called "telephone relay." Instead of passing a baton, you had to shout an assigned seven-digit telephone number to your waiting team member. The team that reached the finish line first and called out the phone number correctly was the winner. The coach had also rigged up a contraption to add wings to our high jumps. First, you climbed atop three sturdy crates, then you jumped onto a trampoline that catapulted you across the bar. It was as close to flying as one can get. All these activities were in preparation for the big parents' day.

The day before the meet, I decided to run the hurdles one more time. I fell and dislocated my left elbow. Mr. Weinberg came running when he heard my screams. Quickly he twisted the arm back into the joint, then called a taxi to take me to the orthopedist.

X-rays showed that he had done a perfect job. Although the bone was chipped, the arm did not have to be reset. I was fitted with a heavy metal splint and a sling and sent home. The next day, I was sitting in the bleachers, watching the competitions, and trying to cheer on my friends. Today my arm is still a bit crooked, reminding me of Mr. Weinberg and the summer of 1938 when I celebrated my thirteenth birthday with the Bar Kochba kids on the field next to the Jewish cemetery in Koenigsberg.

When school resumed in August, the students at the Zickel School began training for the big Sportfest in the Grunewald stadium. Since 1935, the "Day of the Jewish School" had become an annual event in Berlin, and the festival of 1938 promised to be the best yet. Representatives from Jewish schools all over Germany had been invited to compete in Berlin. My friend Hannelore had been chosen to represent Koenigsberg. Organizers of the event sent song sheets to the schools so that every student would join in the singing, and Landsie made sure that we memorized the Hebrew and German texts. Actually, all songs were in Hebrew, except for the two or three composed by Erwin Jospe especially for this occasion.

The festival itself was like a miniature Olympics. After the singing of *Hatikvah* ("The Hope"), the Jewish anthem, the teams of the different schools marched into the stadium. They were distinguished by the color of their shorts—navy blue for the Zickel School, bright green for the Goldschmidt School (their athletes were known as "frogs"), red for the Kaliski School, and so on. There were no official cheerleaders; we all yelled until our voices gave out. The competitions consisted of broad jump, high jump, and sprints (50 meters for girls, 100 meters for boys). There were also shot put and discus events and, of course, the relay races. Between the events, hundreds of students would fill the field with graceful calisthenic exhibitions. When the spectators were not cheering, they filled the stadium with song. After all the winners had been announced, everybody rose to sing *Am Yisrael Chai* ("The people Israel lives forever").

Six thousand young Jews sang in optimistic defiance at the Sportfest in the Grunewald. It was, as one observer noted, one of the very last demonstrations of Jewish vitality before *Kristall-nacht*. After the pogrom of November 9–10, 1938, the Jewish stadium in the Grunewald became a training center for Hitler's storm troopers.

<h1>XIV</h1>

KRISTALLNACHT:
THE NIGHT
OF THE BROKEN GLASS

The Grynzpan family was among the thousands of Polish Jews expelled from Germany on October 28, 1938. They had lived in Hanover, Germany, since 1914, and their children had been born there. One of the sons, seventeen-year-old Herschel, had left Germany earlier and was living in Paris. When he received word from his parents describing the brutal conditions under which they had been trucked to the Polish border and for days had been denied permission to enter, Herschel was seized by an uncontrollable rage. He bought a pistol and went to the German embassy in Paris, demanding to see the ambassador. A minor official, Ernst vom Rath, came out to meet him and was shot by the young man. That was on November 7, 1938.

Hitler threatened that, if vom Rath died, all the Jews would be held responsible and pay for his death. Headlines in the German papers screamed for revenge. I walked around praying that vom Rath would survive. On the afternoon of November 9, 1938, Ernst vom Rath died. A pogrom ensued. The *New York Times* correspondent, Otto D. Tolischus, wrote:

> A wave of destruction, looting, and incendiarism unparalleled in Germany since the Thirty Years' War, and in Europe generally since the Bolshevist revolution, swept over Great Germany today as National Socialist cohorts took vengeance on Jewish shops, offices, and synagogues for the murder by a young

Polish Jew of Ernst vom Rath, third secretary of the German embassy in Paris.

Beginning systematically in the early morning hours in almost every town and city in the country, the wrecking, looting, and burning continued all day. Huge but mostly silent crowds looked on, and the police confined themselves to regulating traffic and making wholesale arrests of Jews "for their own protection."

Ken Dobson, the young Englishman who was teaching at the Zickel School, recalled:

I was aroused from sleep in my room at the Bayerischer Platz by the noise of breaking glass on the night of November 9. It was very quiet outside between the bouts of glass smashing. The next day, lessons were suspended so I went on the tram to north of the city and walked along the Frankfurter Allée and the Warschauer Street, where many poorer Jews lived. I think the smashing of shops was particularly directed at them, as other tactics worked better against the professional class.

When I left for school on the morning of Thursday, November 10, I was not aware of what had happened during the night. I soon found out. When I reached the shopping area near the Bayerischer Platz, I saw the entire sidewalk covered with broken glass. At first I thought there might have been an accident, perhaps a car jumping the curb, but, when I saw the manikins that used to stand in the window of the fur shop strewn around the street, all of them bare and some beheaded, I realized that the glass smashing and looting were part of an organized plan. Every Jewish store in the area had been ransacked. I stepped very carefully, so as not to cut my shoes, and continued on my way.

At school I found chaos. Only a handful of students had arrived. All of them were frightened. Some were crying. Miss Zickel praised us for having come and then sent us home. I walked as quickly as I could. Once more I wished I could be invisible.

The next morning, Friday, November 11, I returned to school. Again there were no classes. None of the male teachers had reported to work. Many of the students who had braved the walk to school told of horrors during the night. Policemen had come to take their fathers away. Some fathers had not come home at all on Thursday evening. "My dad went on a business trip, my mom told me," said one of the girls.

The synagogue on Prinzregenten Street, where my sister had been confirmed one year earlier, had been set on fire. The building, only a few blocks away from the school, was still smoldering. The damp November air smelled of smoke and ashes.

The children huddled in groups in the music room and whispered. Miss Zickel again praised us for having come and offered us chocolate bars as a reward. I didn't feel brave at all and resented the principal's gesture. I had been one of the lucky ones. No Gestapo men had knocked on our door at night and, as far as I knew, my father was safe. Was it perhaps our being so poor that had protected my father? Most of the fathers who had disappeared during the night were professionals. I told Miss Zickel that I did not want the candy and returned it to her. We were sent home again.

During the following days, we learned that 10,000 men had been taken to Sachsenhausen, the concentration camp that was being built in 1935 when I was in Lehnitz. Most of these men were from Berlin and Hamburg. Throughout Germany, 20,000 more had been taken to Buchenwald and Dachau. In some of the smaller towns, all Jewish men, including teenagers, had been arrested. I don't know how the wives and mothers managed to carry on. Many did not know for weeks where their husbands had been taken. Scores received notices to collect packages at the post office. These parcels, containing the ashes of the murdered men, could be claimed for a payment of three marks.

After the Night of the Broken Glass, many Jews from the smaller towns came to Berlin. The big city provided anonymity and welfare organizations. Moreover, the Berliners were known as passive anti-Semites who stood by and watched the destruction and brutality but did not themselves attack Jews, as was the case in the smaller towns. A Jew could still walk on the streets of Berlin without being beaten by the mob.

A relative of my father arrived from Munich. She told us that her husband, a prominent physician, had been shot and killed on November 9. Apparently most of the remaining Jewish doctors in Munich were murdered. Since Jews could only be treated by Jewish doctors, the Munich community was left without medical care.

For months after the Night of the Broken Glass, suicides reportedly accounted for more than one-half of the Jewish burials. The Jewish press was shut down after November 9, and the function of the Jewish Community of Berlin was restricted to carrying out the Gestapo's agenda, primarily in connection with emigration, welfare, and education. Ultimately, the Jewish Community was forced to aid the Nazis in the liquidation of Germany's Jews.

There is ample evidence to support the claim that the excesses of *Kristallnacht* had been organized by Propaganda Minister Goebbels long before the shooting of vom Rath. The purpose of these unspeakable brutalities was to deprive the Jews of their material possessions. The concentration camp victims were forced to buy their freedom by getting out of Germany immediately upon their release. A special exit tax, the *Reichsfluchtsteuer,* was levied on every emigrant whose wealth exceeded a set amount.

It was not enough for the German government to dehumanize 30,000 innocent people. On November 12, 1938, a fine of 1 billion marks (about $400,000,000) was imposed on the Jews as punishment for the death of vom Rath. The storekeepers whose businesses had been ransacked had to repair all the damages. If they had insurance and received any compensation, the money was confiscated by the German government. The Jews had been eliminated from the German economy, lived in virtual isolation, and feared daily for their lives. They had become, in effect, hostages of the Nazis.

But, in November 1938, my classmates and I returned to school to continue our studies. On Monday, November 14, we had classes "as usual." Most of the teachers had returned, as had the majority of the students. Dr. Schwartz, the math teacher, did not come back until the end of the week. It was rumored that he had spent days and nights riding the subways and suburban trains, hopping from train to train to elude the police. They never caught up with him. Visibly aged after his ordeal, Dr. Schwartz plunged into algebra, picking up where he had left off.

When we assembled in the music room, nobody felt like singing. Landsie understood. She taught us a new song:

> My lips are singing,
> My heart in sadness grieves.
>
> That such could be
> I'd never have believed.

Soon everybody was humming and singing. (Nearly forty years later, when my sister Ulla died, I found myself singing this very song. It had surfaced from my subconscious when I needed it.)

A few weeks after *Kristallnacht,* a semblance of normalcy returned. Since most of the synagogues had been gutted, services were now restricted to three buildings on Luetzow, Levetzow, and Kaiser Streets. The altar in the Luetzow Street Synagogue had been damaged, but the building itself was still usable. I returned to services there because I needed to hear the familiar prayers and melodies. The *Kulturbund* (cultural organization) also was active again.

The Gestapo had established a "Central Bureau for Jewish Emigration" in Berlin to expedite the flight of those who had been released from the concentration camps. Several American and British consuls tried to help speed up the emigration process. The British ambassador to the United States offered to relinquish some of the sixty-five thousand quota places allotted Britain in favor of refugees from Hitler. The offer was turned down by the United States government as a violation of the quota law. Jewish organizations proposed a mortgaging of future quotas, suggesting that a three-year allotment of 81,000 be admitted in one year. This plan, which would have saved thousands of lives, also was rejected by the American government. The growing number of applications far exceeded the quota spaces available. In Stuttgart alone, the American consulate received 110,000 applications for the 850 visas it could issue per month!

On January 30, 1939, six years after he had come to power, Hitler promised the Reichstag that the Jews of Europe would be destroyed. There was no reason to doubt his word. Yet, more and more countries restricted immigration of the refugees, condemning thousands of trapped Jews to death.

XV

FAREWELLS

A number of my relatives had the good sense to leave Berlin in 1933. In those days, some people thought that the parting would be temporary. By 1938, however, when most Jews had been deprived of their livelihoods and the possibility of a university education, when Jews were barred from movies, theaters, public libraries, and swimming pools, we tried desperately to get out of Germany. Saying goodbye was a daily occurrence. Of course, we were happy to see that people had been successful in obtaining the required certificates, passports, quota numbers, and visas, and we wished them well. But, at the same time, we were becoming more lonely, more isolated, and less certain of ever seeing our friends and relatives again.

At the Zickel School, Dr. Landsberg taught us songs for all occasions—love and friendship, the joy of meeting, and the sorrow of parting. *Auf Wiedersehen, adiós, adieu, servus,* and *lehitraot* recurred in folksongs, arias, and choral compositions from the Renaissance to the present. Whenever a classmate prepared to leave, we would sing a canon: *Wann und wo, wann und wo, sehen wir uns wieder und sind froh?* ("When and where, when and where, shall we meet again and rejoice?") How often we sang that song!

Some goodbyes were more difficult than others. When Erwin Jospe, the young conductor of the boys' choir of the Luetzowstrasse Synagogue, directed his last Friday night service, the boys, about a dozen of them, ranging in age from about ten to fifteen, were standing in a semicircle, following Jospe's every move with intense concentration. Their voices floated above the congregation, in musical precision and perfect harmony. When they got to the prayer *Uvechen Tzadikim,* they sang with unreserved enthusiasm. The Hebrew prayer books had no translation and the ever present Gestapo agents certainly had no idea what the song signified:

> And, therefore, the righteous shall see and be glad, the just exult, and the pious rejoice in song, while iniquity shall close its mouth and all wickedness shall vanish like smoke, when Thou removest the dominion of tyranny from the earth.

At the conclusion of the service, the young people assembled in an adjoining room for the *Oneg Shabbat,* a brief period of songs, fellowship, and refreshments. These were the moments I lived for. The children were seated at long tables, and each place was set with a small braided roll, a paper napkin, a cup of juice, and a page with the Hebrew words of the "Grace after Meals." The choir boys would rise, and everyone would join in a forceful rendition of *Uvechen Tzadikim* before one of the boys would chant the blessings and we would bite into the rolls. That night, after the Grace, Rabbi Nussbaum told us that this would be Erwin Jospe's last Shabbat in Berlin. He was about to leave for America. Erwin rose and assured us that he would not forget us. "I'll write to you and send you my address," he said, "and, when you come to America, you can look me up." He shook hands with every child and left us each with a word of encouragement.

I left the synagogue sadly and silently and began the two-mile walk home. It was dark, and I walked quickly and resolutely. Suddenly I heard someone crying. Soft sighs became loud, uncontrollable sobs. I saw the assistant choirmaster, a tall boy of about fifteen, walking a few feet ahead of me. He had been very close to Erwin Jospe, his role model and "big brother." Should I run to catch up with him and put my arms around him? Perhaps we could help each other by crying together. Miss Zickel would disapprove, I thought. While I was debating with myself, the boy turned into a side street and disappeared.

After *Kristallnacht,* 1938, emigration reached its peak. Jews emigrated to any country that would open its doors. Sons and fathers who had been released from concentration camps on condition that they leave Germany within one month fled the country, leaving mothers and daughters behind. Sometimes children were sent ahead in the hope that the parents would follow. Sometimes children were sent to live with relatives in Germany while the parents escaped. Families who hesitated, wanting to remain intact, died together in death camps. People left by train or boat, saying their heartbreaking farewells at train stations or the port of Hamburg.

The population of the Zickel School was shrinking daily. Our German teacher, Dr. Kate Laserstein, began assigning essays on personal topics. Perhaps she believed that writing on such themes had therapeutic value. One day she assigned the topic "Parting" (*Abschiednehmen*). It was an experience familiar to all of us and, presumably, an easy one to write about.

I wrote the title at the top of the page and began to organize my thoughts. I started making a list of all the people to whom I had said goodbye recently; I froze, unable to write another word. I looked around the room to see what my classmates were doing. Most of them were filling the pages without looking up. One girl raised her hand and asked if she could write on an alternate topic. "Well," said the teacher, "you may write on anything that concerns leave-taking, such as moving from one neighborhood to another." The girl seemed satisfied and began to scribble away.

I looked at the empty page in front of me. I felt myself getting angry and resentful at being asked to discuss feelings that I had great difficulty controlling. I had maintained a reputation of self-control and stoicism, of being a cool observer. But now I was asked to observe my own painful emotions in a writing exercise. How insulting and humiliating! I looked at the clock and began writing a few sentences explaining why I was unable to complete the assignment. My face turned hot, and I was about to burst into tears. I ran to the front of the room, dropped my paper on the teacher's desk, and stormed out.

The teacher followed me. She looked stunned. "I had no idea that this would upset you so much," she said. "I had to say goodbye to my sister Lotte, who left for Sweden some time ago, and so the topic was very much on my mind."

She never returned my paper, nor did she read aloud or discuss any of the essays. The following week we wrote a description of a painting—a landscape showing a valley before a storm. I had no problem putting my thoughts on paper.

XVI

FATE

On New Year's Day, 1939, I acquired a new middle name. The Nazis decreed that all Jewish females had to add "Sara" to their given names, and all males had to add "Israel." My new name, Marion Sara Freyer, actually sounded quite nice, I thought. Unlike Ulla who had been given the middle name Brigitte at birth, I never had a middle name. The purpose of the additional name, Sara, was not to distinguish me as an individual, however. It was forced on me by the Nazi authorities, and its sole purpose was to mark me as a Jew. Failure to use the complete new name was punishable by law.

For three months, Miss Zickel and a number of faculty members circumvented the rule by signing letters and report cards with their last names only. But, in March, when all Jews had to carry the identity card (*Kennkarte*) bearing the new middle names, Miss Zickel relented and began signing "Luise Sara Zickel," as required. Miss Ollendorff, the French teacher, however, continued to sign her last name only. She was the only faculty member who never revealed her first name. Silently I admired Ollie's spirit of defiance. In the face of dire threats, it took great personal courage to resist the official harassment.

In February 1939, Jews were ordered to surrender all gold, silver, platinum, and precious stones to the authorities. They were allowed to keep only their wedding bands. Again, the majority of German Jews, as law-abiding citizens, followed orders. Some, however, found "legal" ways to disobey the rules. Instead of delivering their treasures to the police, some gave them to non-Jewish friends. Others, who lived in the suburbs or country, buried their candlesticks and heirlooms near some landmark. I know of one refugee family who, many years later, traveled to Germany with their teenaged children to help them discover their roots. They returned to the place that once had been their home and pointed out where they had buried their silver. When they started digging at the very spot, they found, to their amazement, every piece intact, exactly as they had left it.

But these lucky people were a tiny minority. Most Jews could not trust their neighbors or former employees, many of whom were ready and eager to denounce them to the police. And why risk your life for a piece of gold? Our family had no treasures. My mother's plain, gold wedding band became even more precious to her than ever before. She never took it off.

Miss Zickel tried to maintain an atmosphere of "education as usual" after *Kristallnacht*. At school I had to concentrate on irregular French verbs and the theorems of Euclidean geometry. While immersed in texts and tests, I did not sense the anxiety that would come over me at bedtime.

Many nights I would listen for knocks on the door and try to think up an escape plan. "Jump out of the window," I would say to myself, "and then run as fast as you can." Where would I go? Surely, they would catch me. What would happen then? I thought about suicide, a subject discussed openly, especially after we had heard reports of the first returnees from the concentration camps. At night in bed, I would shiver with fright while praying for God's protection. I did not dare discuss my fears with my parents, for I sensed that they shared my insecurity and worries. The morning light revived my courage. Confidently I would gather my books and leave for school.

One afternoon, in January 1939, while walking home from school, I glanced up and saw a familiar face. Hannelore, my friend from Koenigsberg, was running towards me. "What are you doing here?" I gasped in disbelief. "I live around the corner with my uncle and his family," she said. "Can you come home with me? How long will you stay here?" I asked.

As we were walking along Barbarossa Street, Hannelore began

to tell her story: The night after *Kristallnacht,* when the beautiful synagogue of Koenigsberg had been gutted, Hannelore's father and her seventeen-year-old brother, Fritz, were rounded up and incarcerated in different concentration camps. They were promised their freedom on condition that they leave Germany immediately. Hannelore's mother auctioned off all their belongings. The men were released, and the family left Koenigsberg. It was decided that Hannelore would go to Palestine via England to join her sister, who had gone to *Eretz Yisrael* in 1936 with the Youth Aliyah. The parents signed the official papers and left Hannelore in the care of her uncle and aunt on Landshuter Street, about six or seven blocks from our apartment.

"You mean your family left without you? Where did your parents and brother go?" I asked.

Hannelore continued her story: Only yesterday she accompanied her family to the port of Hamburg where they boarded a ship, not knowing which country would admit them. Hannelore said goodbye to her parents and her brother. And, when their ship sailed toward South America, Hannelore boarded a train for Berlin.

From that day until the day I left Germany, I never felt alone. I had a friend with whom to share the ups and downs of life in Nazi Berlin and the secrets and discoveries of adolescence. Together we could cope with restrictions and losses, identity cards, and food shortages. Together we would stand in line for hours and walk away with two bouillon cubes and laugh about it. And, after war had been declared, we braved the blackout together to attend synagogue services. Ours was the friendship of a lifetime.

XVII

DISSOLUTION

In March 1939, in its drive to conquer Europe country by country, Germany occupied the whole of Czechoslovakia. Germany was arming itself at full speed in preparation for war. Eventually Hitler would be stopped, but what would become of German Jewry until that glorious day? Would our family survive?

Our isolation and impoverishment continued. In March, all Jews had to report to the police to be fingerprinted for a special identity card (*Kennkarte*), which assigned a registration number to its bearer. This number had to be cited in any transactions with the authorities. A photo showing the left ear was affixed to the card. Nazi pseudoscientists claimed that the shape of the left ear indicated a person's character and hereditary traits.

The oversized card had to be carried at all times. Because it didn't fit into a regular wallet, we would conceal the card in shoulder bags or in a large pocket sewn into the lining of our jackets. I lived in constant fear of misplacing or losing my identity card. The thought of returning to the police for another card terrified me; I knew that any contact with the Gestapo had to be avoided at all costs.

The *Kristallnacht* destroyed all Jewish retail businesses that had not already been aryanized, depriving even more Jews of a livelihood. Jews were forced to live off their savings or accept support from a special Jewish self-help fund, partially maintained through contributions to the *Blaue Karte* ("Blue Card"). This was the name of the collection scheme for welfare aid. Members of the German Jewish community at large contributed to this fund at regular intervals (I believe it was once a month) to help support the needy and unemployed. As more and more Jews became impoverished, contributions to the *Blaue Karte* decreased correspondingly. By 1939, about one-third of the Jewish population depended on public (Jewish) support.

Through the use of terror and blackmail the expulsion of the Jews was accelerated. For those who had been imprisoned in concentration camps, emigration offered the only road to survival. Even as the Nazis applied tremendous pressure on the Jews to leave, more countries took measures to block their entry. In spite of the obstacles that were put in their way, thousands of Jews managed to get out, legally or illegally, between November 1938 and October 1941, when all emigration stopped.

Rabbi Swarsensky had been among the thousands rounded up during the night of November 10–11 and taken to the Sachsenhausen concentration camp. To comply with the conditions of his release he had to leave Germany within a month. Fortunately, rabbis were exempt from the United States quota system, provided American congregations requested their services. Rabbi Swarsensky went to Madison, Wisconsin, where he established a new congregation, Temple Beth El, which he served for thirty-six years.

I recall vividly the March day in 1939 when Rabbi Swarsensky came to visit my family on Barbarossa Street. I was the one who opened the door for him. He looked a bit thinner than when I had last seen him, but he had the same friendly smile that always put me at ease. When he took off his hat, I gasped at the sight of his shaven head. Noticing my shocked looks, he assured me that his stubble field soon would grow back to normal. He then followed my parents down the long, narrow hallway to the living room. He told us that he had come to say goodbye, that soon he was leaving for America. My parents and sister asked him to relate some of his experiences of the past months. He hesitated at first but then began describing the repeated roll calls where the men had to stand at attention for long periods of time in the bitter cold. He emphasized how lucky he had been to get out of

Sachsenhausen in relatively good health. So many others had been sadistically mistreated, and some had died. He stopped at that point, finding it too painful to talk about the horrors he had witnessed. As the rabbi shook his head in silence, my eyes filled with tears.

My mother asked me to go to the kitchen and brew "substitute" (*Ersatz*) coffee and cut up some fruit for the rabbi. Clearly, she wanted me to hear no more of Rabbi Swarsensky's story. As I walked down the narrow hall to the kitchen, I heard my father laugh. Apparently Rabbi Swarsensky had switched to telling jokes after I had left. I was relieved that he had not lost his wonderful sense of humor.

After the Prinzregenten Street Synagogue was destroyed and Rabbi Swarsensky left Berlin, Ulla rarely attended religious services, but she maintained a lively correspondence with the rabbi. His humorous descriptions of life in America lifted our spirits. We read his letters again and again, circulating them among friends and relatives.

The Jewish population of Berlin kept shrinking. Many of the private schools were dissolved when principals, teachers, and students emigrated. The Zickel School was no exception. On March 31, 1939, we assembled for an emotional closing ceremony. Each class had prepared a different farewell song, which it presented to the whole school. The younger children sang simple folksongs; the senior high school students performed a Mozart choral work. Landsie had reworded the text to apply to our farewell to the Zickel School. She and Dr. Warschauer, the geography teacher, had obtained teaching positions in England. The remaining students and teachers would transfer to other Jewish schools after the spring vacation.

Ulla had now completed her courses at the business college. My parents decided that we should spend the Passover week at my grandfather's home in Koenigsberg. We had celebrated many Passovers with him and my Aunt Kate and sensed that this might be the last holiday we would spend together. Mother packed sand-wiches and apples that sustained us during the ten-hour train trip. We were looking forward to the seder ceremony, which my grandfather would conduct in flawless Hebrew and with great seriousness and dignity. I had practiced the Four Questions, which I, as the youngest participant, was expected to recite.

Although my grandfather did not maintain a traditional house-hold during the year, he did observe all the customs of Passover: stacks of round matzot; the special set of dishes; the table set with white linen, sparkling glasses, and fresh-cut flowers. There would be chicken soup with matzah balls whose recipe had been passed down from generation to generation.

Around the seder table of 1939 sat my grandfather, Aunt Kate, an elderly gentleman from the Jewish community, Ulla, and I. In the past, at least a dozen people had crowded around the table, but, this year, my mother's younger brother, Heinz, and his wife were already in America. Erwin, the other brother, was the legal representative of the Jewish Community of the City of Danzig. He was busy helping Jews emigrate and arranging shipment of the treasures of the Danzig synagogue to New York City for safekeeping. (The *Free City of Danzig*, consisting of the Baltic port and its environs, had been established and named by the League of Nations. From 1920–1939 it was an autonomous state. Germany annexed it in 1939. In 1945, it became Polish again. The Polish name is Gdansk.)

My grandfather recited and chanted the entire Haggadah (story of the Exodus from Egypt) in Hebrew, in a Polish-Ashkenazic accent, while the "audience" sat quietly, except for occasional blessings and responses chanted in unison. I was in awe of my grandfather, surely one of the wisest, most learned, and most generous men I have ever known.

Just as grandfather had finished reciting the Ten Plagues, there was a knock on the door. Was it a Gestapo agent? My Aunt Kate went to the door. "Who is it?" she asked apprehensively. "It's Erwin," a familiar voice replied. The door flung open, and

Erwin walked in. He looked pale and tired. My grandfather put down the Haggadah and said: "I am happy that you came to join us. Sit down so we can continue. We can talk later." He picked up the Haggadah and continued as if nothing had happened. My sister and I were very fond of Uncle Erwin and would have liked to jump up to hug him. But respect for our grandfather did not permit us to interrupt the service.

When we broke for the dinner, my grandfather and Erwin spoke briefly and in whispers. I learned later that my uncle had seen off the first group of Danzig Jews on their illegal voyage to Palestine. At the time Erwin dropped in on our seder, he was still uncertain of the fate of the *Astir* and its passengers.

On April 19, 1939, I started the eighth grade at the Holdheim School. The school, named after Samuel Holdheim (1806–1860), the first Reform rabbi of Berlin, had been in existence for a number of years. Now the Holdheim School gathered in the remnants of the better-known private schools that had closed. I remember that our class had about thirty to thirty-five students. Three of the students had come from the Zickel School, my friends Helga and Daisy and I. Other students had come from the Goldschmidt School and the Kaliski School. The faculty too was composed of teachers who had been left when those schools closed. Dr. Breisacher (history) and Mr. Rewald (art) had come from the Zickel School.

I had no trouble integrating with my new classmates. I was allowed to attend English classes with the rest, and so I discontinued the twice-weekly lessons with my tutor. The atmosphere at Holdheim School was quite different from what I had been used to. The emphasis here was on cooperation and independence, rather than on grades and manners. The principal, Dr. Curt Ofner, who also taught algebra and geometry, often would be called out of the classroom. He would turn to a short boy, Peter, and hand him the chalk. "Take over," he would say as he left. And the lesson continued. I was impressed with the feeling of respect and trust that the students showed toward each other and the teachers.

Our science teacher, Dr. Kurt Neufeld, had been in Sachsenhausen concentration camp. His right arm bore scars from large gashes that ran from his elbow to his hand. The wounds had not healed properly, and the teacher had difficulty holding the chalk. He always had a student assist him with the physics experiments. Everybody in the class admired Dr. Neufeld. More than admiration, it was respect and deep love for a brave man who had survived. A quiet, scholarly man, he was an inspiration to us.

In early June, Dr. Ofner left for England, and Dr. Breisacher, my former history teacher at the Zickel School, took over as principal. The spirit of comradeship continued under his leadership.

On June 28, the school closed for the summer vacation. It reopened in early August, but I did not return. In July, I turned fourteen, and school attendance was no longer compulsory. My father, expecting that we would soon emigrate, took me out of school.

XVIII

KNAPSACKS

Prior to the Hitler regime, there had been a number of liberal, independent newspapers in Germany. The *Frankfurter Allgemeine Zeitung* was known for its staff of outstanding journalists, many of whom were Jewish. When the Nazis dismissed the Jewish writers, Dr. Ernst Breisacher lost his job and became a history teacher at the Zickel School. He presented history as a series of dramatic events, and his entertaining lectures, filled with anecdotes and witty comments, were eagerly attended by the students.

The Nazi propaganda newspaper was *Der Stuermer* (*"The Stormtrooper"*). Its messages of hate, its blatant lies, and its vicious anti-Semitic cartoons could be seen on many street corners, displayed in large glass cases. I wondered if any Jews actually looked as repulsive and grotesque as they were portrayed in *Der Stuermer*. Did its readers really believe that all Jews were criminals and in partnership with the devil?

Since it was impossible to find an impartial account of the news in the German press, many Jews and some of the more enlightened non-Jewish Berliners took to reading foreign newspapers. The owner of the cigar store at the Bayerischer Platz would reserve copies of *The Times* (London) and *Le Temps* (Paris) or the German-language Swiss papers for his regular customers. Since, under Hitler, selling and buying foreign papers was not a patriotic thing to do, the merchant hid these papers behind boxes and files. The initiated knew exactly when they would be available, and the demand always exceeded the supply. I often stopped at the cigar store on my way home from school, hoping to secure a foreign paper. When successful, I would hide it on the bottom of my bookbag and run home with my prize.

For Jews attempting to emigrate, the foreign papers provided the only means to learn about life on the outside. Reports of the debates in the British Parliament concerning Jewish immigration to Palestine and the admission of unaccompanied children to England became vitally important. In the spring of 1939, *The Times* published a large advertisement indicating that the British public was fully aware of the desperate situation of Jewish youth in Germany. The ad showed a number of children sitting on the floor of what seemed to be a railroad station. Each child carried a large knapsack and a round identification label with a name and number. One young girl, her long braids falling over her shoulder, looked straight at the reader. Her sad, dark eyes pleaded for attention. Get Them Out—Before It Is Too Late! read the caption of the ad, an appeal for funds by a Jewish committee for the absorption of the Jewish refugee children.

I remember seeing the ad and feeling encouraged. How wonderful that there were people in the world who cared about us! I knew that Holland, Belgium, and France had opened their doors to Jewish children after *Kristallnacht.*

The Jewish settlers in Palestine offered to "adopt" 10,000 Jewish children from Germany and to receive 100,000 German Jews with productive skills. However, the offers were rejected by the British colonial secretary, who suggested that Jewish children be admitted to Britain, provided their care be guaranteed by Jewish aid organizations. Actually 8,000 unaccompanied Jewish children were allowed into Great Britain after November 1938. But Palestine would remain off limits to Jewish immigration, mainly because of Arab resistance.

Between 1934 and September 1939, the Zionist organization, through its Youth Aliyah program, saved about 3,200 children from Germany and about 1,000 from Austria by transporting them to Palestine. In the early years, the transports were legal, that is, the required immigration certificates had been obtained.

After Britain issued the White Paper in May 1939, and blockaded Palestine, the transports, now illegal, continued. Youths who had been released from the concentration camps were given priority. Only a third of the children who had registered for Youth Aliyah transports could be saved; thousands had to remain behind.

You can imagine how painful and difficult a decision it was for parents to part with their children. In some families, the older siblings were sent away while the younger ones—those under six years of age—stayed with their parents. Most of them would perish.

Dr. Breisacher and his wife had, reluctantly, decided to send their seven-year-old twins, Renate and Hans-Peter, to live with a family in England. I remember visiting the Breisachers in the summer of 1939 in their apartment in Berlin. They showed me the children's room and pointed to a table covered with toys, just as the children had left them. It was almost as if the parents were in mourning. Would they ever see their twins again? Had they prepared them adequately for a life with strangers in a new country with a different language? Would the children remember them?

The family of Joe and Hedy Wolff, like so many others, was waiting for its quota number to be called. Joe Wolff's brother, who had emigrated to New York City many years earlier, had provided the required affidavit. Hedy's younger sister and her family had recently settled in New York. It seemed only a question of time before the family—Joe, Hedy, Hans Bruno, and Marianne—would join them.

But a quota number did not guarantee emigration. After *Kristallnacht*, the Jews lived in constant danger, and they sensed that time could mean the difference between life and death. The war clouds were gathering, and people began to look around for countries to which they could flee on a temporary basis until their number came up. Joe Wolff had business friends in Malmö, Sweden, who were willing to take Hans Bruno (the shy violinist whom I admired from afar) and Marianne for the interim.

In preparation for the future, the entire family was studying English with Ken Dobson—the children at the Zickel School and the parents in evening classes. One evening, in the spring of 1939, Ken Dobson approached the Wolffs after class. He wanted to know if any plans had been made to get the children out of Germany. "Oh, yes," replied the parents, "they will be leaving for Sweden in a few months." Mr. Dobson argued that, surely, if the family were eventually to emigrate to the United States, the children would be better off learning English. To that end he had arranged for Hans Bruno and Marianne to live with his family in Scarborough, England. In typical British understatement, he made it sound so simple and so perfectly logical. All that was needed was the consent of the Wolff parents. "Ma" and "Pa" Dobson had already agreed to take in the Wolff children. The net result of this generous offer was not that the lives of the Wolff *children* were saved, for they would have been safe in Sweden, but that the Wolff *parents* could go to Sweden in place of the children. Thus, the lives of the Wolff *parents* were saved.

In the spring of 1939, Hans Bruno had just turned fourteen, and Marianne was going to be eleven in July. Preparations were made to send the children to England with one of the transports being organized by the Jewish Community of Berlin. There wasn't much to pack. Each child was allowed to carry a knapsack. A small suitcase with items of clothing would be shipped separately. The children were told that the parting would be only temporary. They would go to live with the Dobsons while the parents would soon leave for Sweden to stay with their friends in Malmö. As soon as their quota number would be called, they would all be reunited in America.

A few days before the children's departure, Joe Wolff sat down with his son and explained the facts of life to him. He also reminded him of his responsibilities toward his young sister. Both children were urged to write to their parents every week. On June 5, 1939, Hans Bruno and Marianne waved goodbye to their parents, as the train, packed with Jewish children, pulled out of the train station.

In Berlin, the exodus of Jewish children continued. My classmates, Helga (the school athlete) and Vera (my scholarship partner), left on July 4, 1939, on another children's transport to England. Rabbi Leo Baeck and Otto Hirsch, the leaders of the Jewish Community of Berlin, accompanied one of the last transports. Their friends urged them to remain in England where visas had been granted them. But both men chose to return to Berlin. Leo Baeck had promised that he would not leave Berlin as long as a *minyan* (quorum of ten) remained.

The last children's transport to England left Berlin in late summer. My witty cousin Edith, an ardent Zionist, followed her sister and two brothers to Palestine in August. Hannelore and I drew closer. She had been transplanted from Koenigsberg and was living with her uncle and his family in my neighborhood. We needed each other's companionship and that of other young people. Although all Jewish youth organizations were forced to disband after November 9, 1938, the Zionist groups continued to meet "underground."

Hannelore and I joined a *Habonim* group, which met regularly in private homes. There were about a dozen of us, ranging in age from thirteen to sixteen. It was assumed that everyone in the group would go to Palestine, and the meetings were essentially study sessions to prepare us for life on a kibbutz (communal settlement). Discussions on Jewish themes—books and ideas— were directed by Ruth, our *madrichah* ("leader/counselor"), who was a few years older and spoke Hebrew fluently. We examined the relative merits of living on a small kibbutz versus a large kibbutz, private ownership of tools versus a collective arrangement, and the welfare of the individual in relation to the group. At our clandestine meetings, these serious issues would be debated in hushed voices. There would be no singing lest we attract attention to ourselves. Occasionally someone brought a bag of cookies to share. What a treat! One by one, members of the group left for the training farms (*Probelager, Hachsharah*), which were maintained by the organization. Then they would emigrate with a Youth Aliyah transport. I envied them.

I do not know whether my parents were aware of my involvement with the *Habonim* movement. I did know, however, that they did not share my Zionist ideals. For them, America was the land of promise. As for me, the more I learned, the more I became convinced that Palestine was the only place I could live freely as a Jew. I kept my dreams to myself. The critical goal was to get out of Germany; on that point everyone agreed.

XIX

MOMENTUM

That summer, Hannelore and I helped with the household chores and spent endless hours standing in the food lines. We would walk around the city and join whomever we saw queuing up in front of a grocery store. However, even when items were obtainable, we didn't always have the money to buy them. We usually carried enough change for streetcar fare and a telephone call, but we often spent our few pfennig on rolls or some bouillon cubes and then walked home. My mother had worked out a system of going to the open-air farmers' market just before closing time to buy at bargain prices the picked-over remnants of cabbages and carrots. Wilted cabbage leaves cooked with bouillon cubes and thickened with flour made a tasty soup.

On her way home from school, Ulla had to pass a bakery shop. The odor of freshly baked pastries was irresistible, and Ulla decided to stop in. "Do you have any crumbs?" she asked. The clerk nodded. She twisted a sheet of white paper into a cone and placed it in a glass. With a knife she tapped the empty metal tray to dislodge the crumbs and guide them into the cone. There were particles of donuts, rye bread, and even chocolate cake. "That will be ten pfennig," said the clerk, taking Ulla's carfare. Following the example of my resourceful sister, Hannelore and I made a habit of stopping in bakeries and soon discovered that the crumb harvest was best in late afternoon. Sometimes there was enough for two cones. Then we would walk along the street, savoring the sticky specks of icing and grated nuts that our tongues pried off the soggy paper.

After Ulla had completed her studies at the business college, my father urged her to learn a craft. She enrolled in classes in artificial flower making. The instructors furnished scraps of brightly colored fabrics, plastic pistils and stamens, and the metal templates used to trace the shapes of petals and leaves. With her small, slender fingers Ulla cut, sewed, and glued velvet pansies, silk roses, and dainty chiffon carnations into bouquets that were amazingly realistic. Once again Ulla shared her knowledge with friends who were eager to acquire new skills.

In mid-July of 1939, my father finally received notification from the American consulate that our quota number would be called within a few weeks. Securing the documents needed for our emigration became his full-time occupation. The exodus was gaining momentum.

The German government imposed many requirements before a Jew could *leave* the country, but the United States government presented even greater obstacles for Jews trying to *enter* that country. Section 7(c) of the Immigration Act of 1924 required each visa applicant to furnish a police certificate of good character for the previous five years, together with a record of military service, two certified copies of a birth certificate, and two copies of all other available records kept by the authorities in the country of origin. The law required only "available" documents, but many American consuls insisted upon full files, particularly the police certificate.

It should have been obvious to the United States government and the consuls in Europe that there was little similarity between the conditions of 1924 and those prevailing in 1939. In 1924 Hitler had not yet come to power. Those who left Germany in the twenties emigrated for economic reasons. But those who fled after 1933 did so in order to escape the "extinction of the Jewish race." The flames engulfing the synagogues in November 1938 gave a clear message of Hitler's intentions. How could anyone remain oblivious to the long lines that formed in front of the consulates—lines of desperate people trying to get on waiting lists for quota numbers? Yet the wheels of the bureaucracy continued to grind slowly and inefficiently.

Some Jews dared not go to the police (Gestapo) station to request a character reference. The simple fact of being a Jew made one "an enemy of the German people," as Hitler had repeatedly stated. It seems quite preposterous to have to go to your enemy and ask for a character reference. Thus many were forced to emigrate illegally or not at all.

The *Unbedenklichkeitsbescheinigung,* as the police certificate was called in German, also required statements from the bank and the tax division that no debts were owed. In addition, officers of the Jewish Community of Berlin had to certify that all its tax obligations had been met. A letter from a rabbi attesting to the emigrant's good character was also required. Rabbi Swarsensky sent us such a letter from America.

The necessary documents had to be applied for in sequence and were valid for a limited time. For example, the copies of the birth certificate were needed for the issuance of the *Unbedenklichkeitsbescheinigung,* which was required before a passport could be issued, which was required before a visa could be applied for. Every application meant hours of waiting in line. While I cannot recall all the details, I do remember many days of standing next to my father in lines that wound up and down the staircases in official buildings.

The waiting process could have been accelerated had the United States followed Great Britain's policy of admitting unaccompanied children. As early as January 1939, a group of Roman Catholic and Protestant clergymen had urged the White House to have the country open its door to German refugee children. Senator Robert F. Wagner of New York and Representative Edith Nourse Rogers of Massachusetts introduced identical bills to that effect in the Senate and the House of Representatives. The legislation, known as the Wagner-Rogers Bill or the Child Refugee Bill, stipulated that a maximum of 10,000 children be admitted in 1939, and a similar number in 1940, outside of the regular German quota. The children were to be under fourteen years of age so that they would not be permitted to work. The United States was still recovering from its deep economic depression and did not seek foreigners who would compete in the labor market. The bill further specified that the children would be temporarily adopted by American families and would be reunited with their own parents as soon as conditions were safe. The operation was to be supervised by the American Friends Service Committee.

The response of the American public was quick and positive. Thousands of families of all religious backgrounds volunteered to adopt the children. Some of the leading educators, clergymen, businessmen, and entertainers (Eddie Cantor and Joe E. Brown) tried to use their influence to persuade Congress to pass the bill. Eleanor Roosevelt, who had backed every effort to help the refugees, supported the measure wholeheartedly. Unfortunately, she failed to convince her husband, President Franklin D. Roosevelt, who remained silent. The bill never had a chance; neither did 20,000 Jewish children.

On August 23, 1939, the foreign ministers of Germany and Russia signed a ten-year nonaggression pact. Nobody really believed that this agreement between arch enemies would last. Its immediate effect, however, was to encourage Germany to continue the conquest of Europe unchecked. Hitler was driving the world into war with ever increasing momentum.

My father continued on his rounds of document-gathering. On August 24, we reported to the police to pick up our passports, which had been stamped with the large, red J, identifying us as Jews. It was a big step forward, and we felt like celebrating.

The opportunity presented itself the next day: My uncle Erwin Lichtenstein and his family were passing through Berlin enroute from Danzig to Palestine. I was delighted to see my cousins again. Ruth, now sixteen, got along well with Ulla. Hannah, who was my age, and I had been pen pals for years and were ardent Zionists. Little brother, Hans Walter, was six years old and, of course, the center of attention. My Aunt Lotte, exhausted from the hectic preparations, was happy to turn the little boy over to us. Since Jewish children were no longer allowed to use playgrounds, attend movies, or read in the public library, my father volunteered to take Hans Walter on a subway ride. A fantastic idea! We showed the boy how to coax a ticket out of the farecard machine, and then we held his hand as we waited for the train in the cavernous station. As it came roaring in, we raced for the head car. It was a Saturday morning, and the train was fairly empty. Hans Walter ran to the very front of the car, took his place between my father and the operator's booth, and "guided" the train through the tunnels of Berlin. The sparkling eyes of the make-believe engineer and his shrieks of joy when the train rounded the curves almost made us forget the tensions of the day.

Before we bade goodbye to our relatives, the girls signed my autograph album. Hannah wrote: *Lehitraot be'eretz Yisrael!* ("Until we see each other again in the land of Israel").

On Friday, September 1, 1939, we reported to the American consulate in the hope of receiving our visas. Our documents were checked; we had passed our physical examinations; and then we were told to hand in our passports and return at a later date to pick them up. "We'll come back on Monday," said my father. "On Monday the consulate will be closed," the secretary informed us. "It's Labor Day, an American holiday." We left the consulate somewhat disappointed but still optimistic that, in a few days, we would obtain that all-important visa.

The four of us took the electric city train from the consulate to our home. At one of the stations, a newsboy boarded the train. "Extra, extra!" he called, waving his papers and displaying the headline: German Forces in Poland. England and France Issue Ultimatum. My mother turned pale. "What's an ultimatum?" I asked. "Wait till we get home," my father replied.

I learned that England and France would declare war on Germany unless it withdrew its forces from Poland. And that seemed unlikely. The radio also informed us that the "Free City of Danzig" had been taken by the Nazi forces. Moreover, a curfew affecting the Jews was declared. This meant that, effective September 1, 1939, Jews were not allowed on the streets after eight P.M. in winter and nine P.M. in summer.

On Sunday, September 3, 1939, England and France, as expected, declared war on Germany.

I remember that we greeted this development with mixed emotions. In a large sense, we were glad that England and France had decided, at last, to put a stop to German expansionism. We felt that this move marked the beginning of the end—and the sooner, the better. But we also realized that, under conditions of war, it would be very difficult, if not impossible, for us to get out of Germany. War meant a disruption of all communication with our friends in England, France, and Palestine. From this day on, the children who had gone to England and Palestine on the transports could no longer correspond with their parents. The Times and Le Temps would no longer be available, and the ocean liners that left Le Havre for New York could no longer be reached by the emigrants. I realized that our situation had suddenly deteriorated and felt very discouraged.

On Tuesday, September 5, the American consulate reopened. A new supply of crates of Coca-Cola bottles had arrived ahead of us. We waited anxiously for our turn while the secretaries stopped to smoke cigarettes and drink Coca-Cola. My father reminded me of the American expressions: "Take it easy!" and "Keep smiling!" I did not feel the least bit relaxed or cheerful.

At last, our turn came. The secretary rolled a questionnaire into her typewriter and motioned to my mother to sit down on the chair facing the desk. She asked questions in English and repeated them in broken German. "What was the maiden name of your grandmother?" I heard her ask. My mother wrinkled her brow and hesitated. "I need the maiden name of your mother's mother," repeated the young woman. My mother turned around and looked pleadingly in my father's direction. My father leaned over her shoulder and supplied a name. "We need this information for purposes of identification," explained the secretary. When all forms had been completed, checked, and signed, we were asked to sit in the waiting room.

Finally we were called into the office of the vice consul. Our passports were on his desk. He opened the one belonging to my father and pointed to the page on which a large, rectangular stamp had been printed. It said Immigration Visa No. 5453. Then the vice consul took a pen and signed his name and the date in all the passports, as I watched in awe. When he returned the documents to my father, he smiled. "Congratulations to all of you," he said. "Thank you, sir," my father replied with a sigh of relief.

XX

WAR

And then the lights went out. In September 1939, the days were getting shorter, and the nights were getting longer—much longer. At dusk the streetlights remained unlit. The colorful, illuminated signs on the movies and the cafes stopped flashing. In the apartments, the lamps were moved to the interior while the windows were shrouded with heavy curtains and black paper. The few pedestrians who ventured out after sundown carried flashlights whose lenses were covered with black tape. Through a narrow slit in the cover, a weak ray of light helped spot the greenish reflective paint marking the curbs of the sidewalk.

Detailed instructions showing how to "lightproof" the apartments were given to all Berliners, together with threats of heavy penalties in case the lightproofing fell short of prescribed standards. At the same time, air raid shelters were readied in every apartment building, and a *Luftwart* ("air raid warden") was made responsible for seeing that all tenants followed orders. At the blast of the siren, all residents were to go immediately to the underground shelter and remain there until the all-clear was sounded. We would carry small folding stools down the darkened stairs and huddle in the basement, listening to neighbors discuss the invincibility of the German air force. I remember many sirens and evacuations but not a single R.A.F. (British Royal Air Force) raid. Secretly we hoped that the English bombers would come and blow the Nazis to smithereens.

Even before the declaration of war, all foods and textiles were strictly rationed. Many items were in extremely short supply, especially butter, coffee, and meat. Kosher meat had been unavailable since 1933. Fish had become the main source of protein for many Jews—until they no longer were permitted to buy seafood.

Ulla, who did not "look Jewish," ignored the signs that stated We Do Not Sell Fish to Jews or No Jews Allowed in This Store. Occasionally she would take her place in line with the Aryan customers and triumphantly bring home a piece of herring or flounder. But, after war had been declared, ration cards were required for all purchases, ending Ulla's shopping excursions. Eggs were rationed weekly, one per person. Bottled whole milk was nonexistent; instead, a foamy, bluish liquid that looked like dishwater was dispensed. Cottage cheese, while rationed, was still plentiful and became our main supply of protein. For dinner we often ate boiled potatoes covered with cottage cheese and chives— my favorite dish.

Paper and soap became luxuries. When doing the dishes, I would dip a piece of cork into white sand and use the gritty surface to clean the knife blades. Soap was compressed into a gray, grainy rectangular cake, about $3'' \times 2'' \times 1''$ in size, that lasted a long time because it didn't dissolve easily. We often used white sand to clean our hands, in an effort to conserve soap.

Occasionally, we enjoyed the luxury of real, fragrant toilet soap, thanks to non-Jewish friends courageous enough to help us. Among these "Righteous Gentiles" were Bianca and Siegfried, both professional musicians, who dared ignore the official lies and hatred. Throughout the Hitler years they continued to offer us their warmth and friendship. Bianca had sung leading roles in the opera, but in 1939 she worked part-time in a fancy apothecary shop. Sometimes I would stop in the store to admire the dainty perfume bottles and the imported bath sponges. I would watch Bianca scurrying busily behind the counter, waiting on customers. When everyone had been served and the store was empty, Bianca would hand me a tiny bag and say, "I've held your order. Don't open it until you get home." One day the bag contained not only a piece of soap but a note: "Meet me at the corner at nine tonight."

How could we possibly meet her at nine when the curfew forced us to be indoors by eight? Shortly before nine, Ulla accompanied me to the entrance door of the main apartment building. She would wait for me inside, to help me slip back in on my return. I clutched my blackened flashlight but decided not to use it. Better not attract attention in any way. Gradually my eyes grew used to the dark. I could make out the whitewashed curb and a shadowy figure by the tree. I ran toward the corner. "Here you are," whispered Bianca, as she pressed a flat, flexible package into my hand. She gave me a quick hug. "Run home, dear," she said, as she vanished into the darkness.

That night, we ate fish. The morsels of flounder, brought by a friend who had braved the darkness, became a symbol of love and support to us.

In mid-September of 1939, we observed the High Holidays in Berlin for the last time. Hannelore and I attended services in the Levetzow Street Synagogue. The rabbis were no longer permitted to preach sermons. Since we had to be home by eight, the prayers were brief. We returned the next morning, mainly to show our solidarity with fellow Jews and to sing the familiar melodies. When we came out of the building, we noticed that dried peas had been scattered on the sidewalk. The Nazis wanted us to slip and fall. We walked slowly and deliberately, the young supporting the old. Nobody fell down.

On September 23, we observed Yom Kippur. It was also the day on which all Jews had to turn in their radios at the police station. Sadistically, the authorities had chosen the holiest day in the Jewish calendar to increase our sense of isolation and helplessness.

Preparations for our emigration continued. My parents were busy completing the lists of all goods that we were planning to take to America. Every item, together with its value and date of purchase, had to be recorded on long sheets. These papers, in triplicate, would be taken to the customs office (police station) fourteen days before the two packers and two customs officials

(Gestapo agents) were to come to our house. The date had been set for October 10.

My father briefed us carefully for this important event. At a given signal, my mother was to distract one of the Gestapo agents by luring him into the hall to show him the old sewing machine. At the same time, I was to invite the other Gestapo agent to have a bowl of soup in the kitchen. That would leave my father and Ulla alone with the packers. We rehearsed our roles and were ready when the men arrived.

The Gestapo agents, two middle-aged men, seemed civil and businesslike. The shorter one had a terrible cold and appeared miserable. He was sneezing and coughing and blowing his nose into a large, blue handkerchief. Then he would lay the wet cotton square on top of the radiator to dry. I thought that this practice was most unhygienic and disgusting, but, at the same time, I figured that this man was probably too sick to pay much attention to his job—checking that only those items that appeared on the lists and had been approved by the authorities were actually packed.

My father had been an avid stamp collector all his life, and so he had decided that he would try to smuggle out a part of his collection. He had put the stamps loosely into a shoe box. The idea was to distract the packers and casually slip them the shoe box among the other items. My father was to hold one of the copies of the list and read out each entry while Ulla would hand that article to the packer, who would then put it into the suitcase. The Gestapo agents were to check off the items on their copy of the list. As each valise was filled, the Gestapo men punched two small holes near the handle, passed a wire loop through them, and pressed the ends of the wires together with a metal seal.

The man with the cold was running out of dry handkerchiefs. My father asked me to fix some soup for him. I browned a few cabbage leaves in the heavy skillet and added water, a bouillon cube, and a spoonful of farina. As the cabbage odor filled the living room, my father gave us the signal.

The sniffling man was delighted to follow me into the kitchen. He complimented me on being a good cook and assured me that one bowl of soup would, no doubt, cure his cold. I could hear my mother in the hall, explaining to the other Gestapo agent how to thread the sewing machine. Meanwhile, my father continued to read the lists as Ulla handed the boxes to the packers. At the moment my father asked the packer if he liked cabbage soup, Ulla handed him the illicit shoe box. "This box is so light. What's in it?" asked the packer, suspiciously. "Oh, dear," sighed Ulla, "I must have given you the wrong box," and she quickly handed him an identical shoe box containing some linen napkins and a cake server.

My father opened the door of the living room and shook his head. I realized that things had not gone as planned. The Gestapo men took up their posts again; the "patient" seemed ready to doze off. "Perhaps *you* would like to try some soup?" my father suggested to the other man. I ran into the kitchen to add more water to the pot as I had run out of cabbage. "Put in some parsley and a pinch of dill," said my mother who was an expert at "extending" soups. Then we repeated the entire maneuver. When we returned to the living room, everything had been packed. The Gestapo men sealed the last suitcase and the duffel bag. My father nodded his head and smiled.

We had outsmarted the Gestapo!

After days of waiting in line, my father had been able to book passage on the *Rotterdam* of the Holland-America Line, departing November 16. Since the tickets had to be paid for in dollars, we again appealed to our American relatives for help. Once more they came to our aid. On November 1, 1939, we obtained our exit permits from Germany, valid only from November 1 to November 30. We prayed that nothing drastic would occur (we had been warned that bad things would happen on the anniversary of *Kristallnacht*) to keep us from using these permits—for once they expired, one had to repeat the entire application process. On November 4, my father obtained four railroad tickets for the Dutch train (from Bentheim to Rotterdam) and, on November 11, he went to the office of American Express to exchange ten marks for $2.80, the amount each of us was permitted to take out of Germany. My father was winning the "paper war," and the day of our emigration was fast approaching. "I wish I were seasick already," remarked Ulla.

On November 10, Hannelore and I attended our last Friday night service together at the Levetzow Street Synagogue. After the brief prayers, I bade farewell to the young rabbi. "You are a very fortunate person," said Rabbi Oberlaender, as we shook hands. "I wish I had a chance to get out soon," he added somberly. Suddenly, I felt guilty about leaving behind so many friends and relatives. I realized that Hannelore, who was standing beside me, was still not certain when she would be able to leave for Palestine on a Youth Aliyah transport. The synagogue emptied quickly as the worshipers hurried home to beat the curfew. Most of the "regulars" were elderly people. How many of them would ever get out?

No matter how hard I tried to hide my feelings, I found it very difficult to say goodbye to Hannelore. We promised to write each other very often. We exchanged little souvenirs and vowed never to forget each other.

XXI

THE LONGEST DAY
OF MY LIFE

It really started the night before. On Tuesday, November 14, 1939, the four of us left our apartment on Barbarossa Street to spend the night with acquaintances. We carried with us the sealed hand luggage. Ulla and I had knapsacks on our backs. The larger suitcases and a duffel bag containing two featherbeds and some kitchen utensils had been taken to the railroad station the day before.

I had been looking forward to our emigration for a long time. Whenever one of my friends had left, I tried to imagine what *our* exodus would be like. And now the day had come; it was our turn to leave. There had been so many last-minute preparations that we felt exhausted, physically and emotionally. When my mother suggested that we try to get a night's sleep before the long train ride the next day, we nodded our approval.

I recall that I was asked to bed down on the living room sofa—a loveseat with firm pillows and round upholstery buttons. I spent a very uncomfortable night, tossing and turning, trying to avoid the carved wooden armrests and stone-hard buttons. We arose early. I felt lightheaded and slightly nauseated. The fact that I was menstruating wasn't helping much, and, besides, I had to admit to myself that I was really scared. We had heard rumors of people who had succeeded in getting to the border only to be turned back under some pretext. What would we do if that happened to us?

100

My mother seemed to guess my thoughts. "You must eat your roll," she said. "It will be a long day, and I don't know when we will be able to eat the lunch I packed." My father looked serious, but confident. "I have everything under control," he said. "The most important thing is that you remain silent in the station and on the train. Gestapo agents will be everywhere. One wrong word can make all the difference. Just stay close to me, and do as I tell you."

When we arrived at the train station, my father's mother and his sister, Aunt Paula, were there to greet us. The train, as usual, was exactly on time. My father looked at the tickets and soon spotted the coach on which we had reserved seats. Quickly we kissed our seventy-six-year-old grandmother, who had found a bench to sit on, and promised to write to her often from America. "We'll send you pictures, Omama," said Ulla. Then we hurried alongside the train to our compartment. Aunt Paula helped us lift the luggage as we climbed in.

We leaned out the window. As the train jerked forward, Aunt Paula reached up from the platform, grasped our hands, and said, "Don't forget us." We waved and waved at the slim figure standing on the platform. Then the train turned a corner, and Aunt Paula disappeared from sight.

The train trip from Berlin to the Dutch border took about eight hours. Under normal circumstances, passengers who shared a compartment for an entire day would chat with each other, exchange magazines, or inquire about food in the dining car. But, on November 15, 1939, circumstances were far from normal. The entire train was packed with refugees and Gestapo agents, seated on wooden benches and facing each other, and it was not always possible to tell who was which. For that reason a heavy silence hung over the compartments and the long corridor. The atmosphere was oppressive; the hours dragged on.

Ulla and I left the compartment from time to time and stood by the window in the corridor. We hummed a German folksong as we watched the fields and villages roll by. Both of us were experienced train travelers and had often taken the express to East Prussia, where my mother's father and sister lived. But now we were going in the opposite direction—due west, via Hanover toward Holland, through unfamiliar scenery.

In Hanover, a major transfer point, the train stopped for about twenty minutes. Very few people got on or off. On the platform, vendors hawking Hot Wieners and Hot Broth would stop by the windows so that passengers could buy the food without leaving the train. My father passed a few coins through the window in exchange for cups of steaming broth. It was time to unpack our knapsacks and portion out a sandwich to each. Our provisions were carefully rationed as we wanted to save something for a future meal.

It was late afternoon when we arrived in Bentheim, the German border checkpoint. Since it was wartime and a universal blackout was in effect, there were only a few dim lights in the station. We lugged our suitcases into a closed hall, the size of a large gymnasium, and lined up for the various inspections we had to undergo. There were three crucial tests we needed to pass in order to be permitted to cross the border: the passports and other papers had to be in perfect order; we had to undergo a strip search; and the sealed suitcases had to be opened by the custom inspectors so that the contents could be compared, item for item, with the typed lists that had to be submitted. All these checks had to be completed within a time limit so that we would not miss the Dutch train waiting at the far end of the station.

The refugees rushed to get into line, anxious to overcome these last hurdles. My father did not seem in any hurry. I couldn't understand how he could be so calm when everybody else was so nervous. He took care of the passport inspection for the family, and we were relieved that we had surmounted the first obstacle. Then the four of us were separated for the strip search. All of a sudden I found myself alone and very frightened. After waiting in line, I was asked to enter a wooden booth. A plump, blond woman greeted me and asked me to undress. She examined my clothing, looked between my toes, and then noticed that I was wearing a sanitary pad. "Take that off, I need to look at that," she said. I complied. "What a way to make a living," I thought. "I see you have arch supports in your shoes," said the woman, as she pried the leather pieces apart in search of a forbidden item. "You seem to be all right," she smiled as she returned my clothes to me. "Thank you," I said and made my automatic curtsy. As I got dressed, I thought that this woman probably wasn't really bad. She was only doing her job, like all the others in the German bureaucratic machine. Like all the others, she only followed orders.

When I left the booth, I spied my sister near the custom inspectors. Soon my parents also appeared. I felt I could breathe again. But time was passing, and I urged my father to get in line to have our baggage examined. "Don't rush," he said. "I want to be the last one in line."

At last it was our turn. We had five suitcases and the two knapsacks. As my father handed the custom official our lists, a young woman, clutching the hand of a boy, came running. "I can't find my husband," she cried hysterically. "What am I going to do? He has the papers!" The boy, about four years old, looked at me, his eyes wide with terror. The official shrugged his shoulders. "Mommy, Mommy, find Daddy," sobbed the child as he pulled the woman away from the customs desk. The official counted our bags, looked at the knapsacks, snipped off the seals, skimmed over the lists, and then handed the papers back. "Go on," he mumbled, as he waved us through. My father replaced the lists in his wallet, turned to us, and said, "Let's hurry to the train." We picked up the suitcases and ran to the far end of the platform.

The Dutch train was waiting for us. By now it was evening, and our eyes had to get used to the darkness again. We managed to climb aboard and found upholstered seats in a modern coach. After a few minutes' ride, the train came to a stop at the Dutch border town, Oldenzaal. Dutch officials walked through the train and announced that all passengers had to get off and line up for the passport inspection. My father showed the papers and the reservations for the liner *Rotterdam,* which we were to board the next day, and visas were stamped into the passports permitting us to pass through Holland. Was it possible that I noticed a smile on the face of one of the border patrols? Did I hear the official say, "Have a good trip"?

As we pulled out of Oldenzaal, the lamps flickered and then— *light!* A loud cheer went up; people were embracing and kissing each other. Some began to sing, and there was dancing in the aisles. We had come from darkness into light, from silence to song, from slavery to freedom!

My father found a seat next to me. He leaned close to me. "We can talk now," he said. "We are no longer in Germany! You see," he said, "I wanted to be the very last one in line because I could see that the inspector was getting tired of rummaging through the suitcases. When he saw that nobody was watching him, he just let us go."

I was dead tired and tried to snooze a bit, but the din in the train and the aroma of real Dutch coffee kept me awake. I decided to walk through the train to try to find the distraught mother and her little boy. I walked from one end to the other, past the canteen with the coffee pots, but there was no trace of them.

When we arrived in Rotterdam it was almost eleven o'clock. Hundreds of refugees piled out of the train, carrying their suitcases, knapsacks, and sleepy children to assemble in the large waiting room of the station. There we were met by a representative from the Jewish community. With his neat black beard, narrow face, and dark eyes, he seemed straight out of a Rembrandt painting. After welcoming us to Rotterdam, he invited us to spend the night in a dormitory/shelter provided by the Jewish organization. "That sounds great," I said. "Let's go! I am exhausted." The crowd followed the man with the beard, and soon only a handful of people were left in the station—the four of us among those who had remained. "We won't go to the shelter," said my father. "I'll make some other arrangements." And with these words he walked over to a robust young man who had been helping others with their suitcases.

The young Dutchman had expressed a willingness to find us a

hotel room. The man hoisted one suitcase on his shoulder and carried the other one by hand. It looked easy. My father, Ulla, and I carried the other bags. "I'll show you the way," said the young man. We followed him out of the station into the deserted street. It was chilly and a fine mist enveloped the city. I drew my scarf tightly around my head.

There were a number of hotels near the railroad station, but, at this time of night, their lights were out. The young man knocked on the doors, but nobody answered. We continued walking. My suitcase, filled with books and treasured belongings, grew heavier and heavier. My shoulders ached. I remembered that I hadn't eaten since before we had reached Bentheim, and that seemed ages ago. "I see a light," said the young man, as he set down the suitcases. "You can probably spend the night there." He pointed to a large building on a hill. I read the illuminated sign: German Seamen's Home. "Oh, no," said my mother firmly, "we aren't going there."

It was about 1:00 A.M., and the five of us were still walking along the streets of the misty harbor city. I could smell the dampness. It occurred to me that we were homeless refugees now, without a place to lie down. I was angry at my father for having turned down the offer of the Jewish shelter. We should have gone with the others. What made him think that we were special? How much longer would I be able to keep marching with my books?

"I see light at the Goosen's," exclaimed the Dutchman, visibly relieved. He knocked on the door, and a man answered. Our guide explained the situation, and the man opened the door and let us in. It was Mr. Goosen himself. By chance he had stayed up late to count the day's receipts and enter the figures in his books. He took one look at us and understood.

I have no idea what happened next. The following morning— or was it noon?—I awoke from a coma-like sleep. The blue wool blanket was the softest I had ever slept under. "Get up!" called Ulla, "We are in Rotterdam!"

XXII

HOW DO YOU LIKE
AMERICA?

W e had read about the proverbial Dutch cleanliness and hospitality; now we experienced it firsthand. Mrs. Goosen invited me to take a bath and gave me a large, fluffy towel and a cake of real toilet soap, fragrant and smooth. For days I had not had the chance to wash myself, and a full bath seemed a real luxury. As I was soaping myself in the tub, I felt as if I were washing off the accumulated tensions of the past months and years.

My father had already left to go to the pier. He wanted to make certain that the large pieces of luggage had been loaded on the ship and to determine our boarding time. I joined my mother and Ulla who were having breakfast in the dining room. "Look at that dish of butter!" my mother exclaimed. "Mrs. Goosen has given us a whole week's ration for *one* meal!" "I wish we could share it with Aunt Paula and Omama," said Ulla. We fell silent, thinking that it didn't seem quite right to be eating two soft-boiled eggs each when the people we had left behind were allowed one egg per week.

In Germany, food shortages had occurred as early as 1935 when Hitler decreed that guns took precedence over butter, and the German people went along without complaint. In the winter of 1936–1937, there was a severe butter shortage. At that time we were still living in Friedenau. Across the street from our apartment was a dairy store with a line of customers that stretched around the block. In the late afternoon, Ulla and I would take turns waiting in line. After about twenty minutes of standing in the snow and biting wind, I would lose all feeling in my feet. At that point I would wave my scarf and Ulla, who had been observing the line from the living room window, would come down and take my place. I would return home, thaw out, and then go back to relieve her.

The butter came packed in large, wooden barrels. Clerks would place a piece of wax paper on the scale, dig in the barrel with a wooden spatula to remove a small amount of butter, pat the fat down to squeeze out any drops of water, and weigh out exactly three-eighths of a pound. It was a time-consuming operation, and the line moved very slowly. Ulla and I stayed together as our quest neared completion. When we reached the counter to claim our "prize," we felt a tremendous sense of achievement.

Now we were having breakfast in Rotterdam with Mrs. Goosen urging us to eat as much as we liked. It didn't seem quite real.

In the afternoon, my father returned from the waterfront. "I have news for you," he said gravely. "The large cases and the duffel bag were there, but there was no boat."

"What do you mean?"

"I was told by the steamship company that the British are holding the ship. After all, this is wartime, and England wants to make sure that only friendly vessels sail the British waters. So they are inspecting the liner before letting it enter the Channel."

"How long are they going to keep the boat?"

"The people at the dock couldn't tell me," replied my father. "But they hoped that it would be only a few days."

It could have been worse. The prospect of another night under the soft blue wool blanket was quite appealing. And now that the drizzle had stopped, we decided to take a walk around the city. The main axis of downtown Rotterdam, a wide street called the Coolsingel, was lined with sturdy old buildings, such as the post office, banks, and a large department store, De Bijenkorf ("The Beehive"). The Dutch celebrate St. Nicholas's birthday on

December 5 much as Americans celebrate Christmas, and, since it was November, the store windows were decorated festively. The huge display cases of De Bijenkorf were filled with animated marionettes. There was the shoemaker with the busy little elves, dancing children, and scenes of marionette families feasting at overladen tables. Ulla and I walked from window to window, amidst groups of round-faced, flaxen-haired children who were speaking a strange, guttural language.

My father's trips to the pier became a daily ritual. Day after day he was told that the ocean liner had not yet returned to the home port. At dockside, my father also met some of the refugees who had shared our train ride and who were staying at the dormitory provided by the Jewish community. They had not anticipated spending so many nights in the shelter and were becoming increasingly frustrated with the lack of privacy. I don't think my father revealed our "special accommodations" to them.

Our generous hosts, the Goosens, had made us feel at home, but we were beginning to worry about overstaying our welcome and our inability to pay them for their hospitality. Each one of us had been allowed to take exactly ten marks, equivalent to $2.80, out of Germany. On Sunday, the fourth day of our stay at the hotel, my parents visited good friends who had left Berlin several years earlier and had settled in Amsterdam. These people offered to pay part of our hotel bill. The remainder would be sent from America.

Ulla and I were not able to accompany our parents to Amsterdam. The Goosens, sensing our disappointment, asked us to join their son and daughter for an afternoon at the movies. It was a very special treat for us—for years we had not been allowed to enter a movie theater. The young Goosens—they were about twelve and fifteen—took us on a trolley ride to a theater featuring *Goodbye, Mr. Chips*. The film was in English with Dutch subtitles. Between the two languages I was able to figure out enough of what was going on to cry with the rest of the audience. After the show, our new friends invited us to have ice-cream cones at

De Bijenkorf. I had never tasted anything so rich and smooth, and I didn't expect I would ever again.

As we were going home, we saw a group of Dutch soldiers walking along the Coolsingel. In their trim uniforms they reminded me of the steadfast tin soldier, in Andersen's fairy tale, who fights so valiantly but, in the end, is devoured by flames and melts. Nazi tanks had already overrun a large part of Europe: the Rhineland (in 1936), Austria (in March 1938), Czechoslovakia (in March 1939), and Poland (in September 1939). How long would a handful of Dutchmen be able to resist the onslaught? These thoughts were going through my mind as we returned under the bright lights and holiday decorations of the Coolsingel to Goosen's Hotel.

On Wednesday, November 22, 1939, the British released the liner *Rotterdam,* and all passengers were notified by the Holland-America Line to prepare to board ship that evening. The time had come to say goodbye to the generous and kind Goosens and set out for the pier.

According to my diary, we boarded the ship at 8:45 that evening and bedded down in our tiny cabin. It contained four narrow berths and was equipped with a curtain (no door), a small fan, and a sink. Community lavatories were on each deck.

I had been given the upper berth next to the porthole and watched as the boat left Rotterdam about 3 A.M. We traveled through the canal linking Rotterdam with the Maas River, which empties into the sea. It was a clear, starry night, and I commented in my diary on the lights of the buoys and lighthouses whose reflections seemed to dance on the calm waters. The next morning all passengers had to don life jackets and report for a lifeboat drill. On the distant horizon I could see four huge warships. The steward told us reassuringly that minesweepers would accompany us for protection.

Our voyage across the Atlantic Ocean lasted ten days. Perhaps it was all to the good that the trip took so long. It provided a gradual transition between two worlds. It enabled us to prepare ourselves spiritually for the new life that lay ahead and helped us turn our thoughts from the losses of the past to the challenges of the future.

Passengers on an ocean liner develop a special sense of community. When one keeps meeting the same people at the meals, the lifeboat drills, the entertainment, and the religious services, it is impossible to remain strangers for very long. The Atlantic can be very stormy in November, and in 1939 our ship was bobbing like a cork in heavy seas. On the bulletin board near the entrance to the dining room, our progress was charted on large maps, and the wind velocity was posted. The strength of the wind is measured on the Beaufort Scale, from zero (calm) to twelve (hurricane force). During our crossing, we often reached number nine, a velocity of about fifty miles per hour (strong gale). The activities of the day were also listed on the board, always with the proviso "weather permitting." There was a great deal of seasickness, and, even when entertainment was provided, only a few hearty souls would show up.

The *Rotterdam* was a stately luxury liner now serving as a refugee ship, but the original staff of polite and friendly Dutchmen tried to make life pleasant for us. When the sea calmed down, there were dances to the accompaniment of a live band. One evening, the musicians played nothing but Viennese waltzes in honor of the many refugees from Austria. No doubt they had meant well. But, instead of bringing joy, they brought tears to the eyes of those who had once called Vienna their home. Nobody felt like dancing, for "Vienna, City of My Dreams" had become Vienna, city of nightmares.

Ulla immediately found new friends and showed them samples of the artificial flowers she had learned to make. She had carried the fabric and stencil patterns around with her on the trip. Some of the American passengers ordered velvet and chintz bouquets and paid Ulla in dollars. My sister became the first breadwinner among the refugees on the *Rotterdam*.

I, on the other hand, felt the need to seek out religious activities. Rabbis and professors on board the ship willingly gave lectures on Jewish subjects. In my diary I recorded the Friday night services of November 24 and December 1. Since we were going to arrive in America on Saturday, December 2, on the preceding Friday evening we assembled to recite a special service of thanksgiving for a safe trip and prayers for a safe landing. It was also a last opportunity to say goodbye to Rabbi Rosenthal and the friends I had made among passengers and crew. We had been told that this would be the final voyage of the *Rotterdam*. Upon its return, the stately old liner was to be scrapped.

On Saturday morning, the *Rotterdam* steamed into the harbor of New York. The refugees had assembled on the deck to wave to the Statue of Liberty. I felt I knew her well. She looked exactly like the picture in my textbook, only much larger and even more majestic.

After we had pulled into the dock at Hoboken, New Jersey, our American cousin, Carlos, came on board to meet us. He handed my father a copy of the *New York Times*. "This is the best newspaper in America," he said. And then the debarkation process began: first the American citizens, then the citizens of other countries, and finally the stateless refugees. It seemed to take forever. At last, our passports and visas were checked, and we were permitted to walk across the gangplank toward America. "Welcome!" called a tall man in a uniform. He turned to me. "How do you like America?" he asked. "I *love* it," I replied with conviction, as I set my suitcase on American soil.

Epilogue

The story of the Shrinking Circle did not end with our arrival in the United States. Our thoughts had remained with those we had left behind. Until December 1941, when the United States declared war on Germany, some communication with our relatives in Berlin and Koenigsberg was still possible. We knew that the senders were alive and that they had received most of our letters. But, since all mail was opened and read by Nazi censors, the writers had to be cautious in their choice of words. We learned to read between the lines and to interpret the code words our relatives began to use. In December 1941, all communication from Berlin ceased.

By that time Hitler's armies had overrun most of Europe. Switzerland and Sweden, however, remained neutral throughout the war, and Turkey was neutral until February 1945, when it declared war on Germany and Japan. Friends in the neutral countries acted as go-betweens for Jews in Germany and their relatives in America and Palestine. My grandfather in Koenigsberg maintained some contact with his son, Erwin, in Tel Aviv through a friend in Turkey.

Although we were safe in America, fears for our relatives and friends kept us in a state of constant worry and anxiety. Feelings of guilt and frustration haunted us; we knew that thousands of Jews were being deported to death camps, and there was nothing we could do to save them. By the time the Germans were defeated in the spring of 1945, 123,000 German Jews had been murdered. Six million European Jews, including a million and a half children, perished—one-third of the Jews in the world.

After the war, mail from non-Jewish friends poured in, confirming our worst fears:

My father's mother, seventy-nine years old, had been deported to the East on October 16, 1942, and was never heard from again.

Aunt Paula had been seized at her place of work as a slave laborer on February 27, 1943, and perished in Auschwitz.

Aunt Kate, my mother's sister, died in Lublin in July 1943.

My grandfather died in Theresienstadt in the fall of 1942. On August 25, in terrible heat, he and many of the older members of the Jewish community of Koenigsberg were packed into unventilated cattlecars for the three-day journey to this concentration camp/ghetto in Czechoslovakia. He was eighty-two years old when he died there.

Every year when we celebrate Passover in our home, I see my grandfather and hear him sing "*Dayenu*." We conduct our seder in a more informal manner, reciting the prayers with different accents. But I know that my grandfather is with us—even if he is invisible to everyone but me.

Miss Zickel and her sister were deported to the East in the winter of 1941.

Mr. Weinberg, the gym teacher in Koenigsberg, was unable to get out. He perished.

Dr. Otto Hirsch, executive director of the organization that represented the German Jews (*Reichsvertretung/Reichsvereinigung* [1939]), had accompanied a children's transport to England with Rabbi Leo Baeck. Both men were given the opportunity to emigrate; both chose to remain in Berlin. Otto Hirsch was murdered in June 1941, in Mauthausen, a death camp in Austria.

Rabbi Leo Baeck, head of German Jewry, was deported to Theresienstadt in January 1943. When liberated in early May 1945, he again refused to leave the Jews who needed his help. Two months later, when he saw that the ill were being cared for, he left for London. He died there in 1956.

The Goosens, our generous hosts in Rotterdam, and our friends in Amsterdam disappeared. We surmise that the Goosens were among the 30,000 killed in the bombing of Rotterdam in May 1940. Our Jewish friends were probably among the 105,000 Dutch Jews who died in the Holocaust.

There were times when we hesitated to open foreign mail for every letter told of more deaths: uncles and cousins, well-known rabbis, friends and teachers, whole families and individuals, young and old, those who were killed and those who died by their own hands. The German language newspaper, *Der Aufbau,* published lists of people who were searching for survivors. Whenever we discovered a familiar name among those who advertised, we knew that another individual had escaped.

And, amid all the bad news, there was some good news:

Dr. Kate Laserstein and *Miss Ollendorff* (Ollie) had remained in Berlin throughout the war. They had changed their identities and gone into hiding. When the Allies liberated Berlin in 1945, my teachers surfaced and resumed their teaching careers. Dr. Laserstein's mother, however, perished in Auschwitz.

Lotte Laserstein, the art teacher who had left for Sweden in 1937, was reunited with her sister and Ollie when they came to visit her after the war. She could not persuade them to remain in Sweden. Kate and Ollie returned to Germany where they died, years later, of natural causes. Lotte Laserstein, now a world-renowned painter whose pictures can be seen in museums in London and Washington, and I have begun a correspondence after a fifty-year pause. She is ninety years old.

Dr. Gertrud Landsberg (Landsie), the music teacher, had emigrated to England in August 1939, two weeks before war was declared. She taught French and music in a girls' boarding school. In October 1957, she came to America and settled in California. She died in May 1988, at the age of ninety-three.

Dr. Ernst Breisacher, who had taken over as principal of the Holdheim School, became a college professor in America. The twins, who had gone to England on a children's transport when they were seven, joined their parents after the war.

Erwin Jospe, conductor of the boys' choir, emigrated to America. He served congregations in Cleveland and Chicago and later became dean of the School of Fine Arts at the University of Judaism, Los Angeles. After his retirement, he moved to Israel where he taught music and the opera workshop at Tel Aviv University until his death in 1983.

Hannelore, my best friend, left Berlin with a Youth Aliyah transport on April 4, 1940. During the voyage from Trieste to Haifa, the children changed their German names to Hebrew names, and Hannelore became Tamar. Her Berlin relatives—her uncle and aunt and her two teenage cousins—died in Auschwitz in 1942. Hannelore's parents and her brother, Fritz, had found refuge in Venezuela. They lived in Caracas for two years before emigrating to America where they had many relatives. Fritz joined the U.S. Army and fought in Alsace-Lorraine. In 1945, one month before the end of the war, he was killed. He lies buried in France, not far from Metz.

Bianca and *Siegfried,* our courageous non-Jewish friends, fled Berlin during the bombing raids and survived incredible hardships. After the war, they were able to come to America (California), and we resumed our friendship. "Do you remember how I visited you in the dark?" Bianca wrote me recently. How can I forget?

Hans Bruno and *Marianne Wolff* spent five and a half years at the home of the Dobsons in Scarborough, England. The townspeople had taken up a collection to enable the young refugees to attend high school beyond the compulsory attendance age of fourteen, and both children graduated from English schools. They could not have wished for a more loving, secure home. The Dobsons even provided a violin teacher for Hans so that he could continue his musical studies. And to think that this good fortune had had its beginning in the English classes at the Zickel School! Little Marianne summed it up when she looked up at Ken and said, "At first you were my teacher, then you became my friend, and now you are my brother."

Joe and *Hedy Wolff* waited one year in Sweden for their quota numbers to be called. They then came to America. In January 1945, their grown children, Hans and Marianne, joined them in their one-bedroom apartment in upper Manhattan to begin the third chapter of their lives.

Marion and her family settled in Baltimore. They read *Der Aufbau* regularly in the hope of discovering familiar names in the "In Search Of" and "Just Arrived" columns. When Marion found Hans B. and Marianne listed among the latest arrivals, she contacted them. And that's how it happened that Marion and John (Hans had become John when he served in the U.S. Army) became Mr. and Mrs. Wolff in June 1950.

In March 1975, Ulla died suddenly of a brain tumor. Marion's parents died in 1987. Her father had reached ninety-four years and her mother ninety-two. They had been married for almost sixty-seven years. Uncle Erwin and Aunt Lotte are living in Tel Aviv, surrounded by children, grandchildren, and great-grandchildren. Uncle Heinz and his wife Ursula live in Buffalo, New York.

The circle continues to shrink, but it will never be broken.

Important Dates

January 30, 1933	Hitler comes to power
April 1, 1933	Boycott of Jewish businesses
April 7, 1933	All Jewish civil servants are forced to retire, including all public school teachers, social workers, judges, and court-appointed lawyers
May 10, 1933	Burning of the Books
February 2, 1934	Jews are prohibited from taking the qualifying examinations for physicians and dentists
July 22, 1934	Jews are prohibited from taking the bar examinations to become lawyers
December 12, 1934	Jews are prohibited from taking the qualifying examinations to become pharmacists
July 1935	Marion meets Rabbi Nussbaum in Lehnitz
September 15, 1935	Nuremberg Laws are passed
April 1936	Ulla and Marion leave the public school system to enter the Zickel School
August 1936	Olympic Games in Berlin
May 1937	Ulla's confirmation

March 13, 1938	Annexation of Austria
June 1938	Mass arrests of Berlin Jews
July 1938	Jewish physicians lose licenses to practice
September 1938	Jewish lawyers are debarred
September 30, 1938	Munich Conference Germany annexes the Sudetenland
October 5, 1938	Passports of Jews must be marked with red letter *J*
October 27–28, 1938	Polish Jews residing in Germany are expelled
November 9–10, 1938	*Kristallnacht* (pogrom)
January 1, 1939	Jewish males must add "Israel" as middle name; Jewish females, "Sara"
February 21, 1939	Jews must surrender all gold, silver, platinum, and precious stones. Only wedding bands are exempt
March 1939	Occupation of Czechoslovakia
March 31, 1939	Zickel School closes
April 1939	Last seder in Koenigsberg
May 1939	British White Paper
August 23, 1939	Germany and Russia sign ten-year nonaggression pact
August 24, 1939	Freyer family receives passports
August 25, 1939	Erwin Lichtenstein and family stop in Berlin en route to Palestine

September 1, 1939   Freyer family passes physicals at the American consulate

German forces invade Poland. England and France issue ultimatum

Free City of Danzig is taken over by the Germans

Curfew for Jews takes effect: 8 P.M. in winter, 9 P.M. in summer

September 3, 1939   England and France declare war on Germany. The blackout begins

September 5, 1939   Freyer family receives American visas

September 23, 1939   Last Yom Kippur in Berlin

Jews must surrender their radios at local police stations

October 10, 1939   Gestapo agents seal the suitcases of the Freyer family

November 10, 1939   Marion attends her last Shabbat service in Berlin

November 15, 1939   Freyers leave Berlin for Rotterdam

November 15–22, 1939   Freyers stay at Goosen's Hotel in Rotterdam

November 22–December 2, 1939   Freyers cross the Atlantic Ocean on the *S.S. Rotterdam*

December 2, 1939   Freyer family arrives in America

Bibliography

SOURCES

Baker, Leonard. *Days of Sorrow and Pain: Leo Baeck and the Berlin Jews.* New York: Macmillan, 1978.

Breitman, Richard, and Kraut, Alan M. *American Refugee Policy and European Jewry, 1933–1945.* Bloomington and Indianapolis, Indiana: Indiana University Press, 1987.

Corsi, Edward. *In the Shadow of Liberty: The Chronicle of Ellis Island.* New York: Macmillan, 1935.

Dawidowicz, Lucy S. *The War Against the Jews 1933–1945.* New York: Holt, Rinehart and Winston, 1975.

Deutschkron, Inge. *Berliner Juden im Untergrund.* Beitraege zum Thema Widerstand. Informationszentrum Berlin, 1980. (In German)

Eban, Abba. *My People: The Story of the Jews.* New York: Behrman House, Inc.; Random House, 1968.

Eban, Abba. *Heritage: Civilization and the Jews.* New York: Summit Books, 1984.

Grunberger, Richard. *The Twelve-Year Reich: A Social History of Nazi Germany, 1933–1945.* New York: Holt, Rinehart and Winston, 1971.

Laqueur, Walter. *The Missing Years.* London: Weidenfeld and Nicolson, 1980.

Lichtenstein, Erwin. *Die Juden der Freien Stadt Danzig unter der Herrschaft des Nationalsozialismus.* (The Jews of the Free City of Danzig under the Rule of National Socialism.) Schriftenreihe Wissenschaftlicher Abhandlungen des Leo Baeck Instituts, 27. Jerusalem: Leo Baeck Institute; Tuebingen: J.C.B. Mohr (Paul Siebeck), 1973. (In German)

Lichtenstein, Erwin. *Bericht an meine Familie: Ein Leben zwischen Danzig und Israel.* (Report to My Family: A Life between Danzig and Israel.) Darmstadt: Hermann Luchterhand Verlag GmbH, 1985. (In German)

Morse, Arthur D. *While Six Million Died: A Chronicle of American Apathy.* Woodstock, N.Y.: The Overlook Press, 1983.

Schiller, Friedrich von. *Wilhelm Tell.* Schillers Saemmtliche Werke, Bandt 4. Leipzig: Philipp Reclam (no date). (In German)

Shirer, William L. *Berlin Diary: The Journal of a Foreign Correspondent, 1934–1941.* New York: Penguin Books, 1979.

Swarsensky, Manfred E. *Intimates and Ultimates: A Selection of Addresses.* Madison, Wisconsin: Edgewood College, 1981.

Weisgal, Meyer. . . . *So Far: An Autobiography.* Jerusalem and London: Weidenfeld and Nicolson, 1971; New York: Random House, 1972.

Zweig, Stefan. *Jeremias: Eine dramatische Dichtung in neun Bildern* (A Dramatic Poem in Nine Pictures.) Stockholm: Bermann Fischer Verlag, A.–B., 1939. (In German)

REFERENCE WORKS

Compton's Pictured Encyclopedia, 1959 edition.

Encyclopaedia Judaica, 1971 edition.

The Holy Scriptures According to the Masoretic Text. Philadelphia: The Jewish Publication Society of America, 1951.

Philo-Lexicon: Handbuch des juedischen Wissens (Handbook of Jewish Knowledge.) Berlin/Amsterdam: Philo Verlag GmbH, 1937. (In German)

Philo-Atlas: Handbuch fuer die juedische Auswanderung (Handbook for the Jewish Emigration.) Berlin: Philo GmbH, Juedischer Buchverlag, 1938. (In German)

Wegweiser durch das juedische Berlin (Guide through Jewish Berlin.) Berlin: Nicolaische Verlagsbuchhandlung Beuermann GmbH, 1987. (In German)

Weissensee: Ein Friedhof als Spiegelbild juedischer Geschichte in Berlin (Weissensee: A Cemetery as Mirror Image of Jewish History in Berlin.) Berlin: Haude and Spenersche Verlagsbuchhandlung GmbH, 1987. (In German)

CONTRIBUTIONS TO YEARBOOKS OF THE LEO BAECK INSTITUTE

Freeden, Herbert A. "A Jewish Theatre under the Swastika." *First Yearbook of the Leo Baeck Institute.* London: East and West Library, 1956.

Mayer, Paul Y. "Equality-Egality—Jews and Sport in Germany." *Twenty-Fifth Yearbook of the Leo Baeck Institute.* London: Secker and Warburg, 1980.

Strauss, Herbert A. "Jewish Emigration from Germany—Nazi Policies and Jewish Responses (I)." *Twenty-Fifth Yearbook of the Leo Baeck Institute*. London: Secker and Warburg, 1980.

PERSONAL LETTERS AND COMMUNICATIONS

Kenneth Dobson, England. Letters dated 8/21/86, 1/3/87, and 4/1/87.

Charlotte Gerson (nee Lotte Weihrauch), Missouri, U.S.A. Letter dated 11/26/86.

Rabbi Alfred Jospe, District of Columbia, U.S.A. Letter dated 8/18/86.

Tamar Peled (nee Hannelore Winterfeld), Israel. Letters dated 7/27/86 and 9/30/86.

Bianca Schultze, California, U.S.A. Letter dated 2/8/87.

Helga Stummer (nee Helga Edelstein), Canada. Letters dated 7/27/86 and 9/30/86.

Marianne Wolff, M.D. (Mrs. Herbert Schainholz), New Jersey, U.S.A. Letter dated 1/5/87.

Poem Recited by Ulla at Her Confirmation, May 1937

Das sind nicht wir,
Das ist das Judentum worum es geht
Im Kampfe aller Rassen.
Das sind nicht wir,
Das ist das Heiligtum um das es geht,
Um Liebe oder Hassen.
Das sind nicht wir,
Denn dieser Kampf waer Nichts,
Wenn es um Menschen geht
Die sterblich sind.
Es geht um die Idee des Ewigen Lichts,
Mit dem Es endet, mit dem Es beginnt.

Und dieses Es, das grosse, Ewige Sein
Ist wert, dass Millionen dafuer leiden.
Es ist der Morgen, ist der Fruehrotschein,
Der letzte Trost, wenn wir vom Leben scheiden.
Das ist das Wunderbare
Das die Welt erfuellt mit Glanz und alter Sage,
Dass, wenn auch alles rings in Truemmer faellt,
Ein Licht noch strahlend macht die Nacht zum Tage.

Und dann ist Eins das unsre Tage lenkt,
Fuehlbar in uns
Das unsichtbare Wesen
Das sich uns selbst als hoechstes Glueck geschenkt,
Von dem wir in den alten Buechern lesen.
Denn hinter dieser Macht steht mehr als das
Worum es geht im Kampfe aller Rassen.
Es ist der Kampf der Liebe mit dem Hass.
"Du, segne mich, ich kann Dich doch nicht lassen!"

Wir Menschen, nur vergaenglich wie ein Licht,
Wir kaempfen jetzt
Und unser ist ein Leiden.
Ein Schmerzensmal schreibt sich auf das Gesicht,
Ein Schmerzensmal vom Alltag uns zu scheiden.
So musst Du's sehn.
Das ist das Judentum worum es geht im Kampfe dieser Tage.
Es geht um unser Enkel Heiligtum.
Und sieh,
Die Traene rinnt.
Stolz schweigt die Klage.

Author unknown

Glossary/Index

Adass Yisroel: Orthodox, independent religious society, founded in 1869. Not part of the Jewish Community of Berlin, 26

Affidavit: A sworn statement in writing, made under oath. In particular, a legal document signed by an American citizen, guaranteeing that the immigrant would not become a public charge, 51, 52, 58

Aryan: Original meaning: a member of the Indo-European-speaking people. Under Hitler it came to mean a Gentile of nordic-German background; a member of Hitler's master race, 13, 21, 27

Auschwitz (Oswiecim): Extermination camp in southern Poland, near Krakow, vii, 114

Baeck, Rabbi, Leo (1873, Lissa–1956, London): Rabbi of the Jewish Community of Berlin, 1912–1943. Leader of the Jews of Germany. Deported to Theresienstadt in 1943, liberated in May 1945. Emigrated to England, 29, 85, 113

The Leo Baeck Institute, 129 East 73rd Street, New York, N.Y. 10021: Founded in 1955 as a repository of books and archives concerning the life and history of German-speaking Jewry from its beginnings to its end under the Nazis. There are branches in London and Jerusalem.

Bar Kochba: Jewish athletic organization, 58, 59

Bianca and Siegfried: Non-Jewish friends in Hitler's Berlin, 95, 96, 115

Blaue Karte ("Blue Card"): Plan by which members of the Jewish community contributed monthly to a welfare fund to help impoverished fellow Jews, 75, 76

Breisacher, Dr. Ernst: History teacher at Zickel School, principal of Holdheim School in spring 1939, 79, 80, 81, 83, 114

Brie, Mr.: Owner of notions store in Berlin-Friedenau, 1–2

Buchenwald: Concentration camp in southwest Germany, near Weimar, 64

127

Confirmation of Ulla, May 1937, 32–34, 124–125

Consul: An official appointed by a government to reside in a foreign country to represent the interests of the appointing country, 88

Consulate: The offices of the consul and his staff, 52, 88, 91, 92

Crystal Night: See *Kristallnacht.*

Dachau: Concentration camp in Bavaria, near Munich, 64

Danzig, Free City of (Gdansk): Established by the League of Nations in 1920 and annexed by Hitler in 1939, 78, 92

Day of the Jewish School: Annual sports event in which athletes from Jewish schools competed. It took place in the Jewish stadium in the Grunewald, near Berlin, 60

Dobson, Kenneth: English teacher at the Zickel School; foster brother of John and Marianne Wolff, 42, 63, 84

Elternhilfe ("Parents' Aid"): Organization set up by the Jewish Community of Berlin to provide financial aid to deserving Jewish high school students, 41

Emigration: The act of leaving one place of residence to live elsewhere; usually leaving one country permanently to establish residency and citizenship in another country, 44–49, 57, 66

Freyer:
  Eva Lichtenstein (author's mother, 1895–1987)
  Flora Lewinsky (grandmother, 1863–1942)
  Leo (father, 1893–1987)
  Marion (author)
  Paula (aunt, 1895–1943)
  Ulla (Ursula) (sister, 1921–1975)
Friedenau: Working class suburb of Berlin, 1, 15, 27, 40, 41

Gemeindeblatt: Periodical published by the Jewish Community (*Gemeinde*) of Berlin, 26

Gestapo: German Secret Police (*Geheime Staatspolizei*), viii, 27 passim

Goethe, J. W.: German poet (1749–1832), 30, 37

Goldschmidt School: Jewish private school in Berlin, founded and directed by Dr. Leonore Goldschmidt, 60, 79

Goosen Family: Owners of Goosen's Hotel in Rotterdam, 105–109, 113, 114

Grynszpan, Herschel: Jewish youth who assassinated Ernst vom Rath, an official at the German embassy in Paris. This event provided the pretext for the *Kristallnacht* of November 9–10, 1938, 62

Habonim: Labor Zionist youth organization founded in 1935, 85, 86

Hannelore: Marion's best friend, 59, 60, 73, 74, 85, 87, 96, 99, 115

Hatikvah ("The Hope"): Text by Naphtali Herz Imber set to music by Samuel Cohen. Zionist anthem, 1898; Israeli anthem, 1948, 60

Hebrew Language: The language of the Jewish people since biblical times. The national language of the State of Israel.

Heine, Heinrich (1797–1856): Jewish poet, 30

Hirsch, Otto (1885, Stuttgart- 1941, Mauthausen concentration camp): Executive director of the *Reichsvertretung* (National Council of German Jews), 85, 113

Hitler, Adolf (1889–1945): Dictator of Germany, founder of the Nazi party, 1, 4 passim

Hitler Salute (*Heil Hitler!*): Military salute, rendered standing, with outstretched right arm, viii, 6

Holdheim School: Private Jewish secondary school in Berlin, founded by the Reform movement, 79

Holocaust, The: The period of 1933–1945 in which six million Jews perished under Nazi rule, vii passim

Identity Card (*Kennkarte*): Required to be carried by all Jews, beginning in March 1939. Contained photograph, finger prints, and serial number, viii, 72, 75

International Rescue Committee: Organization that rescued about 1,500 Jews after 1940, 51

Jeremias: Drama by Stefan Zweig, published in 1917, 37, 47–48

Jospe, Erwin: Director of Boys' Choir at the Luetzowstrasse Synagogue; music teacher at the Kaliski School in Berlin, 60, 68, 69, 115

Kaliski School: Private Jewish secondary school in Berlin, 60, 79

Kennkarte: See Identity Card.

Koenigsberg/Pr.: University town in East Prussia. After World War II it was renamed Kaliningrad, 11, 57, 59, 60, 73, 74, 77, 112

Kristallnacht ("Night of the Broken Glass"): The night of November 9–10, 1938; the organized pogrom on that date, marked by the burning of synagogues, smashing of store windows, looting of stores, and the imprisonment of 30,000 Jewish men and boys to concentration camps, 61, 62–67, 75

Kulturbund (Jewish Cultural Organization): Founded in 1933 by Dr. Kurt Singer. Active until September 11, 1941, 36–38, 66

Landsberg, Gertrud: Music teacher at Zickel School, 39, 57, 60, 68, 77, 114

Laserstein, Kate: Teacher of German language and literature at Zickel School, 57, 70–71, 114

Laserstein, Lotte (sister of Kate): Portrait painter, art teacher at Zickel School, 71, 114

Lehnitz: Camp/Resort/Meeting House, northwest of Berlin, maintained by Jewish Community of Berlin, 8–11 passim

Lichtenstein:
Erwin, Dr. Jur. (uncle of author)
Heinz, M.D. (uncle)
Johanna Samuel (grandmother, 1861–1935)
Kaethe (aunt, 1890–1943)
Max, Dr. Jur. (grandfather, 1860–1942)

Lyck/Pr.: Town in East Prussia, birthplace of Leo Freyer, 50

The Magic Flute: Opera by W. A. Mozart, 39

Makkabi: Jewish athletic organization, 19

Mosaic Religion: Judaism, 4

National Council of Jewish Women: Founded in 1893 for the study of Judaism and the rendering of social service, 50, 52

Nazi: Refers to the N.S.D.A.P., the National Socialist German Workers party (*Nationalsozialistische Deutsche Arbeiter Partei*), 2, 3 passim

Neufeld, Dr. Kurt: Science teacher at Holdheim School, 80

Nuremberg Laws: Passed on September 15, 1935, legitimized racial anti-Semitism, deprived Jews of German citizenship and all government jobs, 13

Nussbaum, Dr. Max (1910–1974): Rabbi of the Jewish Community of Berlin, 1935–1940, 9– 11, 28, 29, 69

Ofner, Curt: Principal of Holdheim School, 79

Oldenzaal: Dutch border checkpoint, 104

Ollendorff, Miss: Teacher of French and gym at Zickel School, 20, 72, 114

Olympic Games, summer of 1936 in Berlin, 19–21

Oneg Shabbat: Fellowship and refreshments after the Friday night service at the synagogue, 17, 69

Oral History Project of the Jewish Community Council of Greater Washington: Records experiences of survivors and liberators, vii

Oranienburg: Small town northwest of Berlin. Site of the Sachsenhausen concentration camp, 8

Owens, Jesse: Sprinter, gold medal winner in the 1936 Olympics, 21

Passover: Jewish festival commemorating the Exodus from Egypt. Festival of spring and freedom, 77–79

Pogrom: Russian word meaning "riot" or "devastation," used to describe all violent anti-Jewish attacks.

Portner, Annie: Gym teacher at Zickel School, 20

Pfefferkorn, Dora: Elementary school teacher in the public *Volksschule* in Friedenau, 4–7, 14

Prinz, Dr. Joachim (1902–1988): Rabbi in Berlin, 1926–37. President of the American Jewish Congress, 1958–66, 28

Prinzregenten Strasse Synagogue: The last synagogue built on German soil, Berlin, 1930. It had 2,300 seats. Destroyed November 9–10, 1938, 27, 28, 32, 64, 77

Quota Laws: Regulations limiting entry into the United States by establishing maximum annual levels of immigration from each European country, as well as various qualifications for immigrants, 50–52, 67

Rabbi: Teacher, spiritual leader of a Jewish congregation. Role of the German rabbis under Nazi rule, 26–29

Rath, Ernst vom: Third secretary in the German embassy in Paris in 1938, 62, 63, 65

Rebecca: Author's daughter, vii, viii

Reichsvertretung: The National Council of German Jews, organized in September 1933, with Rabbi Leo Baeck as president and Otto Hirsch as executive director. Its purpose was to represent the Jewish legal interests to the German government, 13, 19, 113

Reichvereinigung: As of April 7, 1939 the name of the *Reichsvertretung*. Its stated purpose was to encourage emigration of the Jews and supervise the Jewish schools and Jewish welfare system in Germany, 113

Riley, Miss: English teacher at Zickel School, 42

Rotterdam: Port in Holland. Name of the ocean liner on which the Freyer family sailed for America, 98, 103, 104, 107, 109, 110–111, 113, 114

Sachsenhausen: Concentration camp near Oranienburg, northwest of Berlin, 9, 80

Schild: Jewish athletic organization, 19

Schiller, F. von (1759–1805): German poet and dramatist, 6

Schwartz, Mr.: Mathematics teacher at Zickel School, 66

Seder ("order"): The ceremony/meal conducted in Jewish homes on the first two days of the Passover holiday. (See Passover.)

Shavuot: Jewish festival celebrated seven weeks after Passover commemorating the giving of the Ten Commandments and the first harvest, 32

Simchat Torah ("Joy of the Law"): The joyous festival of completion of the reading of the Five Books of Moses, marked by singing and processions, 27

Singer, Kurt, M.D. (1885–1944): Neurologist, musicologist, conductor, and cofounder of the *Kulturbund,* 36, 38

Stadium in the Grunewald: Athletic stadium owned by the Jewish Community of Berlin, 20, 60–61

Suicide: The act of terminating one's own life. During the years 1933–1943, many Jews chose suicide over torture and murder by the Nazis, 44 passim

Swarsensky, Dr. Manfred (1906–1981): Rabbi in Berlin, 1932–1939, 28, 29, 32, 33, 47, 76, 77

Synagogue: Jewish house of worship. Its role in the Jewish Community of Berlin under Hitler, 26–29

Tarnkappe: Mythical hat that renders its wearer invisible, vii

Tell (*Wilhelm Tell*): Drama by F. von Schiller, 6, 7

Theodor Herzl School: Private Jewish high school with a Zionist orientation, Berlin, 10, 13, 15

Theresienstadt (Terezin): Town in Czechoslovakia. Originally housing 8,000 people, it was turned into a "model" ghetto, housing about 68,000 at one time. Of the 200,000 Jews sent there, an estimated 120,000 were deported to Auschwitz and between 33,000 and 40,000 died in Theresienstadt. Leo Baeck is one of its famous survivors. (See Leo Baeck.) 11, 29, 38, 113

Ulla: Sister of author (1921–1975), 3 passim

Unbedenklichkeitsbescheinigung: Character reference required by the United States for emigrants from Europe, 89

Wagner-Rogers Bill: A congressional bill introduced in February 1939 by Senator Robert F. Wagner (Democrat of New York) and Representative Edith Nourse Rogers (Republican of Massachusetts) to bring into the United States 20,000 German refugee children during a two-year period, outside the quota. The bill died in Committee, 89–90

Warschauer, Dr. Martin: Geography teacher at Zickel School, 57, 77

Weimar Republic: A constitutional republic established in 1919 with Friedrich Ebert as president. Ebert died in 1925 and was succeeded by Hindenburg. The appointment of Hitler as chancellor on January 30, 1933 marked the end of the Weimar Republic, 11

Weinberg, Mr.: Physical education teacher in Koenigsberg, 59, 60, 113

White Paper of 1939: British official document imposing strict quotas on Jewish immigration to Palestine and an absolute ban on land sales to Jews, 28, 83

Wiener, Dr. Max: Rabbi and historian in Berlin, 28

Wolff:
Joe (father-in-law of author, 1892–1973)
Hedy (mother-in-law, 1898–1978)
Hans Bruno (John) (husband)
Marianne (sister-in-law)

Youth Aliyah: Jewish organization that rescued about 10,000 Jewish children from death in Europe and resettled them in Palestine, 16, 59, 74, 82

Zeiss Optical Company: Manufacturer of precision instruments for Hitler's war efforts, Friedenau, 40

Zickel, Luise: Founder and director of the Zickel School, a Jewish private school in Berlin, 16, 17, 41, 42, 63, 64, 69, 72, 73, 113

Zionist: Originally, a person who supported the establishment of a Jewish national or religious community in Palestine. Now, a supporter of the State of Israel, 9–11, 15, 16, 28, 47, 58, 82, 85

Zweig, Stefan (1881, Vienna–1942, Brazil): Jewish writer and dramatist, 37, 47